24K PRAISE FOR
THE PLATINUM RULE

"Fun and useful insights as to how to enhance both business and personal relationships. Tony Alessandra is a master of this and I recommend that you read it often."

—Jack Canfield, co-author of *Chicken Soup for the Soul*

"Great book! Lots of practical information....Teaches you how to surprise the customer and lead the competition. It's worth more than gold for anyone in business."

—Robert Kriegel, Ph.D., co-author of *Sacred Cows Make the Best Burgers*

"Help [for] those who want to increase their sensitivity to others and their power to communicate."

—*Publishers Weekly*

"Fascinating....Easy to read....Helpful and empowering information is encompassed in this great book."

—Les Brown, CPAE, author of *Live Your Dreams*

"Dr. Tony Alessandra's work brilliantly provides effective insights for improving communication in any and all situations. Everyone will benefit from reading THE PLATINUM RULE."

—John Gray, Ph.D., author of *Men Are from Mars, Women Are from Venus*

"Pure business gold....Entertaining and thought-provoking....An impressively effective, proven technique for gaining power and influence in the workplace."

—*Business Times*

"Insightful, spiritual, and practical, all packed into one powerful book."

—Wayne Dyer, author of *Your Erroneous Zones*

"The most important, practical, and effective book ever imagined. Everyone should read it!"

—Brian Tracy, author of *Maximum Achievement*

more...

"Buy this book. Read it. Become its student and put its extraordinary technologies to use immediately for platinum results."
—**Tod Barnhart, author of** *The Five Rituals of Wealth*

"THE PLATINUM RULE is a must-read for all of us who want to be better in our interactions with others."
—**Ken Blanchard, co-author of** *The One-Minute Manager®* **and** *Everyone's a Coach*

"You'll recognize yourself and all your contacts immediately. THIS platinum will be your most precious natural resource."
—**Kathy Levine, host, QVC, Inc.**

"THE PLATINUM RULE breaks all the old rules of communications. It is full of take-action strategies. Don't underestimate the power of this fine book. A learning and earning tool for the times."
—**Harvey Mackay, author of** *Swim with the Sharks without Being Eaten Alive*

"This simply written but special book is a true treasure. A great book!"
—**Og Mandino, author/speaker**

"If you want to become a better salesperson, negotiator, and communicator, read THE PLATINUM RULE. It's the key to getting others to do what you want."
—**Michael LeBoeuf, author of** *How to Win Customers and Keep Them for Life*

"A valuable guide to understanding the human resource."
—**Charles Garfield, Ph.D., author of** *Second to None* **and** *Peak Performers*

"A quantum advance in identifying personalities. Practical yet powerful advice."
—**Dr. Anthony Wild, CEO, Parke Davis**

"Must reading for all management."
—**Jeff Olson, president & CEO, The Peoples Network**

"Teaches us all how to effectively manage people."
—**Raymond Zimmerman, chairman & CEO, Service Merchandise Co., Inc.**

"This approach to dealing with people has been instrumental in our success. It really works!"
—**Lou Alesi, president & CEO, InterMetro Industries**

"A must-read for people who are in sales and marketing and people who need to deal with customers day in and day out."
—**Bob Russell, president, The McGraw-Hill Companies**

"An extremely useful and illuminating book on leadership styles—but, more important: a book that will give all managers some important insights about themselves."
—**Warren G. Bennis, distinguished professor and founding chairman of USC's Leadership Institute, and author of** *On Becoming a Leader, An Invented Life* **and** *Why Leaders Can't Lead*

"THE PLATINUM RULE will work wonders while you're 'working' any room. If someone isn't your type, it will help you figure them out and insure your communication success."
—**Susan RoAne, author of** *How to Work a Room, The Secrets of Savvy Networking,* **and** *What Do I Say Next?*

"[THE PLATINUM RULE] is the priceless key to empowerment, productivity, and all business and personal relationships....It is simply the most important leadership concept I have learned in all of my life!"
—**Denis Waitley, author of** *Empires of the Mind*

"THE PLATINUM RULE is a blueprint for getting everything you want. As you read this magnificent book, you'll learn how to make your world work for you."
—**Mark Victor Hansen, co-author of** *Chicken Soup for the Soul*

"A practical—and powerful—tool for interacting with others."
—*Working Solo Newsletter*

"A book that should be on everyone's reading list...simple [and] intuitive....Goes far beyond its genre to touch issues central not only to business, but to any area where personal relationships are involved. This is a book for anyone interested in service to others."
—*Book Scapes*

ALSO BY TONY ALESSANDRA

Non-Manipulative Selling
(with Phillip S. Wexler and Rick Barrera)

The Art of Managing People (with Phillip L. Hunsaker)

Selling by Objectives (with Jim Cathcart and Phillip Wexler)

The Business of Selling (with Jim Cathcart)

Be Your Own Sales Manager
(with Jim Cathcart and John Monoky)

People Smarts (with Michael O'Connor and Janice Van Dyke)

Publish & Flourish (with Garry Schaeffer)

Idea-a-Day Guide to Super Selling and Customer Service
(with Gary Couture and Gregg Baron)

Communicating at Work (with Phil Hunsaker, Ph.D.)

Collaborative Selling (with Rick Barrera)

ALSO BY MICHAEL O'CONNOR

People Smarts (with Tony Alessandra and Janice Van Dyke)

Mysteries of Motivation (with Sandra Merwin)

Managing by Values (with Ken Blanchard)

THE PLATINUM RULE

DISCOVER THE FOUR BASIC
BUSINESS PERSONALITIES—
AND HOW THEY CAN
LEAD YOU TO SUCCESS

Tony Alessandra, Ph.D., and
Michael J. O'Connor, Ph.D.

WARNER BOOKS

A Time Warner Company

Warner Books, Inc. 1271 Avenue of the Americas, New York, NY 10020

Visit our Web site at http://warnerbooks.com

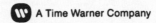 A Time Warner Company

Printed in the United States of America
First Trade Printing: February 1998
10 9 8 7 6 5 4 3 2 1

Library of Congress Cataloging-in-Publication Data

Alessandra, Anthony J.
the platinum rule : discover the four basic business personalities—and how they can lead you to success / Tony Alessandra and Michael J. O'Connor.
p. cm.
ISBN 0-446-67343-9
1. Interpersonal relations. I. O'Connor, Michael J., 1944— II. Title.
HM132.A3546   1996
302—dc20   95-52491
                                           CIP

Book design by Giorgetta Bell McRee
Cover design by Jon Valk

I dedicate this book to my family:

To my wife, Sue, for her encouragement, support, and love;

To my parents, Margaret and Victor, for their teachings and guidance;

To my children, Justin and Jessica, for their love and faith in me;

To my step-children, Ashley and Dana, for their acceptance of me; and

To my brother and sister, Gary and Linda, for their admiration and loyalty.

TONY ALESSANDRA

This book is dedicated:

To my family—present, past and emerging—whose personal belief in, and commitment to, the principles embedded in **The Platinum Rule** has provided me with the energy and conviction to push onward;

To my friends whose support has enhanced my life through their sharing, supportiveness, and coaching direction;

To the many "teachers" who were so generous and precious in sharing the wisdom that has been so critical to my own continuing learning; and

To those many colleagues and clients whose own ongoing use of **The Platinum Rule** has enriched both themselves and others with the gifts of greater joy, peace, and genuine success.

MICHAEL O'CONNOR

Acknowledgments

This book has been a team effort. Some people contributed content either directly or indirectly, and others provided useful input about the manuscript.

We wish to thank Katherine Briggs, Jim Cathcart, Roger Dawson, John Geier, Paul Green, Phil Hunsaker, Carl Jung, Florence Littauer, William Marston, David McClelland, David Merrill, Isabel Briggs Myers, Janice Van Dyke, and Larry Wilson for their research and writings.

Those who gave valuable feedback on the manuscript include Jim Cathcart, Jeff Davidson, Phil Hunsaker, Nikki Sweet, and our valuable editor at Warner Books, Susan Suffes. We thank you all very much.

Special thanks go to all of the authors, business people, and celebrities who read the manuscript and provided the powerful endorsements that appear on the covers and front pages of this book.

We gratefully thank our literary agent, Margret McBride, who pushed and guided us for over four years until we had an acceptable proposal. Only then did we start writing the book.

Finally, we owe a great debt of appreciation to Dale Fetherling whose incredible writing skills made this book fun to read, easy to understand, and such a practical tool for all of us to use.

TONY ALESSANDRA
MICHAEL O'CONNOR

CONTENTS

1

◆

HAS THE GOLDEN RULE
LOST ITS GLITTER?

• You're such a terrific salesperson you could probably sell a stethoscope to a tree surgeon. But from the moment you greet this prospective client, it's obvious he doesn't like you, isn't about to like you, and wouldn't do a deal with you if you were giving the product away.

• The conference is packed; you don't know a soul. But then you bump into a stranger and—*wow!*—it's as if you've been friends forever. Everything that's said and done meshes magically.

• As manager, you're fired up about the new program and eager to inspire your employees. You call them in one by one and give them the same lively motivational pitch that so excited you. But you're astonished when their reactions vary from enthusiastic to tepid to hostile.

1

PERSONALITY DIFFERENCES

Personality differences are our boon and our bane. They're what makes life so rich and fascinating—and often so frustrating, too. Especially at work, where teamwork and motivation are pivotal.

Most of us never figure people out. We just ricochet through life. We get along great with some people, refuse to deal with others, or have as little interaction as possible with still others, because they're so—well, *different*—from us.

But what if you knew the secret of those differences? What if there was a simple, but proven, way to build rapport with everyone? To eliminate personality conflicts? To take charge of your own compatibility with others? To make business mutually beneficial instead of a contest of wills?

You literally hold such a key in your hands. A product of psychological research and practical application, **The Platinum Rule** is a proven method of connecting with anyone in the workplace and is indispensable to anyone who's curious about what makes themselves and others tick.

You can learn to handle people the way those people want to be handled, to speak to them in the way they are comfortable listening, to sell to people the way they like to buy, to lead people in ways that are comfortable for them to follow.

In business, especially, people all too often create tension and discomfort by assuming we're all pretty much alike. In fact, most of us, if asked about a philosophy of personal relations, probably would recall

The Golden Rule, which we learned as kids: "Do unto others as you would have them do unto you."

THE DOWNSIDE OF THE GOLDEN RULE

That's an old and honorable sentiment. A lot of good has been done in the world by people practicing The Golden Rule. As a guide to personal values, it can be a powerful force for honesty and compassion. But as a yardstick for communication, The Golden Rule has a downside.

If applied verbatim, it can backfire and actually cause personality conflicts. Why? Because following The Golden Rule literally—treating people the way *you'd* like to be treated—means dealing with others from your own perspective. It implies that we're all alike, that what I want and need is exactly what you want and need. But of course we're not all alike. And treating others that way can mean turning off those who have different needs, desires, and hopes.

Instead, we suggest honoring the real intent of The Golden Rule by modifying that ancient axiom just a bit. We think the key to lasting success in business, and the secret to better relationships, is to apply what we call **The Platinum Rule**:

"Do unto others as *they'd* like done unto them."

That means, in short, learning to really understand other people—and then handling them in a way that's best for *them*, not just for us. It means taking the time to figure out the people around us, and then adjusting our behavior to make them more comfortable. It means using our knowledge and our tact to try to put others at ease. That, we suggest, is the true spirit of The Golden Rule.

So **The Platinum Rule** isn't at odds with The Golden Rule. Instead, you might say it's a newer, more sensitive version.

TELEGRAPHING YOUR PERSONALITY

At the root of **The Platinum Rule** is this: Each person has his or her own habits and his or her own way of looking at the world. Those recurring traits fall into fairly predictable patterns, known as behavioral styles or personal styles.

Each of us telegraphs our personal style by the way we shake hands, how we react to stress, the way our office looks, how we make decisions, whether we're crisp or chatty on the phone—and in many other ways. The skill is in learning to spot those signals, identify the other person's style, then adjust our own behavior to lessen conflict.

IDENTIFYING THE STYLES

People have been frustrated and fascinated with one another's differences for thousands of years. Starting with the early astrologers, theorists have sought to identify these behavioral styles. In ancient Greece, for example, the physician Hippocrates outlined four temperaments—Sanguine, Phlegmatic, Melancholic, and Choleric—and in 1921, famed psychologist Carl Jung, the first to study personal styles scientifically, described them as Intuitor, Thinker, Feeler, and Sensor.

Since then, psychologists have produced more than a dozen models of behavioral differences, some with sixteen or more possible personality blends. Sometimes the styles have been given abstract behavioral-science names, and sometimes they have been named after birds, animals, or even colors. But a common thread throughout the centuries is the grouping of behavior in four categories.

We want this book to be readable, practical, and accurate. What's more, we want you to be able to remember the principles of **The Platinum Rule** easily. So we're using a simple, four-style model that spans all cultures and has been validated with hundreds of thousands of people. It focuses on patterns of observable, *external* clues that will give you a sense of what's going on *inside* someone else's head. Once you know that, you can decide how best to respond.

We've given the personality groups simple, descriptive names. Under **The Platinum Rule**, then, everyone basically exhibits one of these styles:

- **Directors:** Firm and forceful, confident and competitive, decisive and determined risk-takers. While their impatience sometimes causes eyes to roll, the Directors leave no doubt who sits at the head of the table.

- **Socializers:** Outgoing, optimistic, enthusiastic people who like to be at the center of things. Socializers have lots of ideas and love to talk, especially about themselves.
- **Relaters:** Genial team players who like stability more than risk and who care greatly about relationships with others. They're likable but sometimes too timid and slow to change.
- **Thinkers:** Self-controlled and cautious, preferring analysis over emotion. They love clarity and order but may come across as a bit starchy.

As you'll see, natural allies and enemies abound among the various styles. But here's the bottom line: *Your communication is only as good as your understanding of the person you're communicating with.*

This book will teach you to become a people-watcher extraordinaire, someone who really understands personality differences—and can use them to mutual advantage. This can often spell the difference between success and failure. Two examples:

A mortgage broker had a client who'd earlier had some bad experiences with salespeople. Each time the broker set up meetings with her, she made up a last-minute excuse to postpone. Finally, he got to see her. Applying **The Platinum Rule** principles, he figured out her personal style, adapted to it, and closed the deal. She told him, "When I made the appointments, I dreaded each time the date neared. But I actually had a wonderful time. You really made learning about the loan process interesting, and I trust you. You have a gift for communication."

At last report, the broker had gotten four referrals from the woman—*and he hadn't even finished her refinancing.*

> An entrepreneur approached another friend of ours with a business proposal. The entrepreneur is extremely outgoing and animated, fond of hearty, two-handed handshakes and calling people loudly by their first names and asking about their spouse and kids, whom he often barely knows. Our friend is a terrific businessman, but he's more of a team-builder: warm but restrained, pleasant but not pushy. He's more into genuine dialogue than slaps on the back.

Can you guess the outcome? There was enormous tension. Both were uncomfortable and, of course, they couldn't reach an agreement—for reasons having nothing to do with the facts of the proposal.

It could have been different. If either had practiced **The Platinum Rule**, he could have changed his behavior a bit to make the other person more comfortable. They could have created a bond and maybe made a deal.

INFINITE USES

So the uses of **The Platinum Rule** are infinite. This book will show you how to placate the customer who's got not only a gripe but an attitude. It will tell how to fire up the overly cautious co-worker, bring the perfection-bent loner onto the team, and work with the executive who has trouble making a decision. You can learn to handle the domineering boss, the gregarious colleague who spends more time gabbing with co-workers than dealing with clients, and the leader who's got a zillion ideas but no follow-through.

You'll learn how to build bridges to each style in any work situation: asking for a raise, closing a sale, planning a big project, providing better service, or building morale.

As a result, **The Platinum Rule** can be your key to:

- Stronger career prospects
- Higher productivity
- Greater satisfaction
- Improved customer relations
- Fewer conflicts and less tension

In fact, at work and elsewhere, **The Platinum Rule** will likely change your relationships forever. You'll see people differently, understand them better, and be able to deal with them in a way that can turn every encounter into a win-win situation.

Also, perhaps for the first time, you'll truly understand your own personality and why you act the way you do. You'll see how to round off your own sharp edges and to develop strengths you didn't know you had.

Some people reject the notion of "types" or "styles." Putting people in boxes, they say, is not the way to really get to know one another. Instead, they contend, that's stereotyping, a process that may be unfair to the individual and uses unrealistic shortcuts to appreciating unique human beings.

But understanding someone's behavioral style *isn't* mutually exclusive with genuinely getting to know them. Far from it. In fact, using **The Platinum Rule** can greatly accelerate that process. If you can quickly pick up on another person's needs-based cues and adapt your own behavior, you'll learn to value others more genuinely. You'll see that their needs are just as valid as yours, and you can, if you choose, seek to meet those desires and forge a deeper relationship.

Throughout this book you'll also see that we urge you to improve your listening skills—and we give you pointers on how to do so. Good listening enriches relationships and, in tandem with **The Platinum Rule**, can help build a lasting rapport that is anything but superficial.

NOT MANIPULATION

Another important point: When we talk about using **The Platinum Rule**, we're *not* talking about manipulating people! Rather, we are talking about learning, in a way, to speak their language.

It isn't considered manipulative to speak French when in Paris, for example. *Au contraire.* It's something you do briefly while on the Frenchman's soil so you can be more compatible. You don't alter your basic nature while in France. Your ideas don't change. But *how* you present those ideas does change.

Similarly, practicing **The Platinum Rule** doesn't fundamentally change you or the other person. It empowers you by making you multilingual, in a sense. Knowing how to listen and speak in the "language" of those around you is a delightful, useful tool that can be used to resolve differences, maximize strengths, and enjoy a fuller, more successful life by better understanding yourself and the people around you.

2

♦

GETTING TO KNOW
THE FOUR BASIC STYLES

Your phone rings. Ralph, one of your department heads, says he's coming right over with a problem that's "Urgent!" He sounds so upset you fear he's on the verge of an emotional meltdown.

Okay, before he gets here ask yourself, What are the ways I might handle this?

• *Ralph may need someone to reach out to him.* So be gentle and understanding to a good employee who's having a bad day. Calmly listen while he gets this crisis off his chest.

• *He may need backbone.* Get a quick grasp on the problem, then give him a goal. Ask him to come up with options.

• *Ralph may need clarity and order.* So go over the details with him. Help him make sure he's not overlooking something.

• *Or maybe he needs camaraderie.* Then forget the details! Remind him that the job is supposed to be *fun*.

Trade a few stories, assure him that "we'll work it all out somehow."

These are four very different approaches to appeal to four different behavioral styles. But if Ralph's like most people, only one approach will work with him. How do you decide? Do you just guess—and run a 75 percent chance of making Ralph feel worse, not better?

Hardly.

In fact, you're very confident. That's because you know and practice **The Platinum Rule**. So you're certain you'll be able to give Ralph the reception he needs and deserves.

The Platinum Rule tells you to handle Ralph not the way *you'd* wish to be treated, but the way *he* wants and needs to be treated. After all, his hopes and fears and dreams are likely different from yours.

And here's the best part: Ralph unknowingly sends you signals every day telling you just how he wants to be handled. So there'll be very little guesswork. You've been observing Ralph, and you *know* his personal style.

You swear by **The Platinum Rule**. It's been an invaluable tool for you. In fact, it's given you a skill with people that's cited as one of the big reasons why you're sitting in the boss's chair.

TAKING CHARGE OF COMPATIBILITY

We all face such people-handling choices constantly. Whether we're a leader or the led, a peon or a potentate, a seller or a buyer, we make crucial decisions about how to treat people. That's life. And, especially, that's business, where our success depends on the web of relationships we build. Most of us don't build that web very systematically. We are naturally drawn to some people, are indifferent to many, and repelled by yet others, usually for reasons we don't fully fathom.

But you can take charge of your compatibility. You can connect with everyone in the workplace. In fact, **The Platinum Rule** will allow you to understand anyone on the planet. Once you know a person's style, you can choose to adjust your own behavior in a way that makes that person comfortable. When others are comfortable with you, trust, communication, and credibility soar.

OUR STYLE IS OBVIOUS

There are four distinct behavioral styles. But only one slips on as smoothly, as naturally, as a good-fitting glove.

Many of us are blends of styles, yet we still have a dominant one, and we can't hide it. Whether we're male or female, young or old, at the top or the bottom of the pecking order, are a part of a Western culture or some other, our personality style is obvious.

Now it's true, we don't always act the same. You behave differently with your best friend, say, than with your boss. You don't act at a picnic as you do at a funeral. But we all display mostly one style most of the time.

Your style may have its own particular twist. But it's still clearly one of the four basic styles, just as a song may be interpreted differently by various singers but is clearly recognizable as the same tune.

We all send out signals revealing our style. Which words you choose, your body language, the speed and rhythm of your speech, for example. How you dress, how your office is organized, how fast you walk. You also send signals by how openly you share your feelings, how quickly you make decisions, and how eagerly you embrace change.

So the signs are numerous. But if you know them and can interpret them, you'll soon recognize your behavioral style—*and* everyone else's. Then you can:

- better understand and accept yourself;
- behave in a way that will improve compatibility with anyone; and
- improve your productivity and career prospects.

THREE IMPORTANT POINTS

In this chapter, we're going to meet the four basic personal styles. But before we do, please understand that:

1. These are not judgments. None of these styles is the best, or better than another. All have their pros and cons, as we'll soon see.

2. Learning to read others' personal styles will give you an enormous advantage in dealing with them.
   Not because you're going to manipulate them!
   Not because you can convincingly change your personal style the way you change your socks!
   But because you *can* learn to slip into the other person's frame of reference. You can see through the other person's eyes long enough for him or her to accept you, rather than making him or her defensive.

3. Understanding the four basic styles will allow you to read and respond to others, thus reducing friction. But, importantly, having this skill will also help you see why *you* do what you do. That reduces friction, too.

Now let's find out about those four basic behavioral styles, their strengths, their weaknesses, and how people with each style think. We'll learn their worst fears, biggest assets, greatest failings, and what most excites them. Plus, you'll see how each might tackle important tasks, whether it's painting the ceiling of Rome's Sistine Chapel or preparing a jetliner for take-off.

THE DIRECTOR

Move Over and Let the Big Dog Drink

A family crisis. A corporate takeover. Or just figuring out how best to split a restaurant tab. It makes no difference—Directors dive in headfirst as if they, and they alone, have the answer.

We all know Directors and admire them—even as we cringe. Awesome at their best, insensitive at their worst, they are the dominant, driving people we often think of as "natural leaders." They are not shy or, usually, modest. They often make good football coaches, army generals, and dictators.

Challenge-oriented and decisive, they are propelled by an inner need to be in charge. The key to a good life for them is achieving, overcoming obstacles, accomplishing things.

If Michelangelo had been a Director, here's how he probably would have gone about painting his famous frescoes on the ceiling of Rome's Sistine Chapel:

Make a quick sketch, tell the Vatican to back off, hire a crew to put up the scaffolding, and then delegate the painting to half a dozen other artists who would give him a daily progress report showing how many square feet were being covered each day. He'd review their work, adding in his own final touches.

This would give him control, yet still free him to line up bigger challenges, such as, say, St. Peter's Basilica.

Would the finished ceiling have been a work of art? Well, maybe, or maybe not. But, for sure, the job would be done competently, come in under budget—and on time!

☑ *What excites them? Action*

Because they feel so strongly about winning and overcoming obstacles, Directors are not afraid to challenge people or rules that seem to stand in their way.

They are often highly territorial. Control and endurance are their favorite tools, and one-upmanship can be a lifelong hobby.

More interested in meeting their goals than in pleasing people, they often end up on top—alone.

☑ *Greatest Asset: Out-Accomplish Anybody*

Directors are the people about whom it's often said enviously, "He makes things happen" or "She definitely gets things done."

High-energy people, they seem to fill up a room just by walking into it. Independent and very competitive, Directors demand—and get—results.

These people can move mountains. Others are in awe of their vitality, decisiveness, and ability to figure out quickly what needs to be done—and then just *do* it.

They're able to focus intently and are very task-oriented. One Director has his secretary fax his mail to him when he's out of town so he can return to a totally clean desk.

More than any of the other three types, they like change and initiate it the most. They're not afraid of risk. They work quickly and impressively by themselves, juggling multiple tasks.

They love to work hard. They often thrive on crises and controversies. They like to display their killer instinct and beat long odds.

If a project is group-oriented, the Director is comfortable delegating, but only if those below him produce results, not just talk.

☑ *Greatest Failing: Can't Stand Weakness*

Directors are frequently frustrated when others aren't as able or motivated as they are. And they're not good at hiding that frustration. So they may look at or speak to non-Directors in a way that suggests they're dummies.

Directors are the kind of people who think nothing of straightening out pictures in other people's houses. Or commenting with utter bluntness on how others dress: "That's a nice color on you. Too bad they didn't have your size."

They may take themselves too seriously. Directors can benefit from gentle reminders to laugh at themselves, or to slow down and take time to smell the flowers.

But even if they heed that advice, their competitiveness runs so deep that they may return and say to others, "I smelled twelve flowers today. How many did you smell?"

☑ *Greatest Fear: Being "Soft"*

Directors like to deal quickly with practical problems. Down deep, they know they could get better, faster results if only they could get people out of the way.

They're rarely interested in abstract ideas. Similarly, they tell others flat out what to do rather than communicating obliquely.

They're impatient. They're the kind of people who love the VCR because it allows them to speed through television commercials. One Director we know can't bear to buy a green tomato.

Directors see themselves on a logical road toward corporate advancement. In fact, they can envision themselves rising to become el numero uno—the best, or maybe even the best *ever*.

It's not a matter of *if* the Director will take over, but *when*. The brassy Directors may push you around as much as you'll allow them to. And even at a round table, they leave little doubt in your mind about who sits at its head.

They're very much into efficiency, and into gadgets that promote efficiency. More than any other personality type, they're likely to call you from their car phone.

Directors, however, are not into praise. About the only time you're likely to hear them say "Well done!" is when they order a steak.

THE SOCIALIZER

Let Me Entertain You

If Directors are mountain climbers in an endless quest for new peaks, Socializers are more like entertainers always in search of a good time and a good audience.

A chatty, expressive, fun-loving optimist, the Socializer likes to ride the crest of ideas, causes, or projects that come, one after another, like waves. Any one wave may not last long, but it can be a great ride—especially if the beachgoers cheer.

Socializers love people and thrive on being where

the action is. Long on ideas, short on follow-through, the Socializer leads by dealing with others in an up-beat way. Fast-paced, energetic, and outgoing, the Socializer's innate belief is: If he can show you that he likes you, you'll follow him.

They may do well in public relations or as salespeople, entertainers, or, say, cruiseship social directors.

The key to the good life for the Socializer is building a network of friends and admirers who will appreciate his or her flair for fun and creativity.

If Michelangelo had been a Socializer, here's how he probably would have gone about painting his famous frescoes on the ceiling of Rome's Sistine Chapel:

He'd talk about lots of ideas, but he'd have no single plan. He'd start in one corner and just wing it, painting whatever struck his fancy as he chatted merrily with anyone who was around.

His work would show flair and style. He would have a good time and probably even make some new friends as he interrupted others to tell stories and show off the sections he'd just completed. When it was all done, he'd throw a huge kick-off celebration—and sell postcards of the finished ceiling.

Would the painting be a masterpiece? Well, perhaps in the conception, if not in the execution. But in either event, the Vatican still would be talking about what a great guy that Michelangelo was!

☑ *What Excites Them? Tossing Around Ideas*

More than any of the other three types, Socializers seek admiration and acceptance. They also want to make work fun. One Socializer pulls a football out of his desk drawer during crises and whips spiral passes around the crowded office. It results in greater acceptance from other Socializers—and a lot less from non-Socializers who have a different idea of a "fun" workplace!

Generally speaking, Socializers are generally speaking. They love to talk and to be talked about. If you don't talk about them, they may spend considerable time talking about their favorite subject: themselves.

☑ *Greatest Asset: Fun to Be Around*

Socializers are enthusiastic, playful, and persuasive. They show their feelings openly and frequently.

They know no strangers. Socializers will brainstorm with virtually anyone they meet. Very expressive, they sometimes say too much—and to the wrong people.

Highly intuitive, they come up with lots of ideas, some practical, some not. They judge those ideas by whether they *feel* right. They then seek results by persuading others to get on the bandwagon.

☑ *Greatest Failing: Being Erratic*

Socializers sometimes display the attention span of a flashbulb, especially when stressed out. They tend to speak before thinking. In fact, their thoughts can be like gumballs coming out of the vending machine: They just sort of fall to the tongue and then roll out.

Easily bored and always needing new stimulation, Socializers may make big decisions based on scant data.

They love ideas but hate the routine of putting them into practice. So they often start projects and then look to someone else to finish them. Or they'll get so many projects started at once that they face an impossible deluge of deadlines.

The Socializer likes to use stories and jokes when making a point or issuing instructions. But being such a smooth talker, he or she can seem evasive or come off as a phony. And they may tend to procrastinate because dealing with a lot of details just isn't very exciting to them.

☑ *Greatest Fear: Not Being Liked*

Not as task-oriented as Directors, Socializers crave approval more than achievement. So they're much more emotional and people-focused in their decision-making.

The Socializer also is the most spontaneous of the styles. At its best, there's a childlike quality to their impulsivity. To the Socializer, the joy of discovery is half the fun—whether it's in a disorganized office or in a free-floating mind.

Socializers see themselves as "big picture" people, and thus prefer to avoid lots of specifics. Planning and follow-through aren't enough fun to be high priorities.

Deep down, the Socializer wants companionship—and recognition from those companions!

THE RELATER

It's not whether you win or lose,
it's how many friends you have.

Please make a note: If you are taken hostage by terrorists, pray that your negotiator is a Relater. He or she will be low-key, calm, and discreet, unlikely to make any sudden moves or say anything that will anger your captors.

In fact, Will Rogers might have said, "I never met a Relater I didn't like." Almost everyone likes them, and Will Rogers himself probably *was* one.

Friendly and personable, they operate at a slow, steady pace and seldom show emotional peaks or valleys. These easygoing folks are comfortable as teachers, counselors, clergy, and in customer-service roles.

The key to the good life for them is being a long-time member of an ongoing team that proceeds slowly and methodically.

If Michelangelo had been a Relater, here's how he probably would have gone about painting his famous frescoes on the ceiling of Rome's Sistine Chapel:

First, he'd listen to Vatican officials at length about what exactly they'd prefer in a mural and what his relationship with them would be before, during, and after the project. Then he'd gather a loyal support staff, making sure they all had the right brushes, paints, and enthusiasm.

After drawing up a step-by-step plan, he'd request that they work as a team, using identical colors and even standardized brushstrokes. Once they began, he'd see to it that they all persevered until every last smile was in place on every last cherub.

Would the ceiling be a work of art for the ages? Possibly. Some critics might say it lacked panache. But others would laud it for being done earnestly, methodically, and thoroughly. And members of the team would swear it was the most fulfilling experience of their lives.

☑ *What Excites Them? Productive Routine*

More than the other three types, Relaters yearn for tranquillity and stability. They have already made their life's One Big Decision: to try to avoid making

25

many big decisions. They prefer to walk solidly down the middle of the road.

Relaters are pleasant, cooperative team players. They have a strong need to belong. You're likely to see lots of family- or work-related photos on their desk; nearby walls may be decorated with key mementos of affiliations (work and personal) and experiences.

Relaters make changes slowly and only after much thought about the effect on others. Being good listeners, Relaters always find time for friends; being dependable employees, they quietly do what they're told, even if they disagree.

They pride themselves on being "realistic." One Relater still plays tennis with the boss who fired him.

Rocking the boat, or aggressive behavior of any kind, is a turnoff. But Relaters probably won't articulate that, either, because they're so mild-mannered.

☑ *Greatest Strength: Easy to Get Along With*

Relaters have "laid-back" dispositions. They accept people as they are. They care deeply about feelings, yours and theirs. But not being as assertive as the Socializer, the Relater is less likely to speak about those feelings.

Relaters are steady, competent—not flashy—employees. They are much better at detail and follow-through than Socializers and much more tolerable than Directors. In fact, they often get promoted because they have so few enemies.

The Relater is inherently modest. Unlike the

Socializer or Director, he or she views actions as speaking louder than words. "Be ready" is their watchword, and proven procedures are their gospel. So they're likely to gather all their thoughts first, collect needed tools and materials, unfurl the plans, and then—only when it's clear that everything's in its place—begin work. (Many a Director or Socializer might scorn such elaborate preparation, yet marvel later at the Relater's consistent, predictable output.)

☑ *Greatest Failing: Timidity*

Relaters are in love with routine. Often initially reluctant about new projects, or change in general, they must be convinced that the opportunity outweighs the risk.

They detest conflict. They're easy marks for door-to-door solicitors, or for bosses seeking "volunteers" for undesirable duty.

Unassertive and sensitive, they may go along with others, even if they don't agree. Or they may settle for present conditions even if change is clearly needed.

☑ *Greatest Fear: Change*

Relaters want stable relationships that don't put anyone on the spot, especially themselves. So they often avoid giving direct commands. Instead, they veil their suggestions or orders in anecdotes or illustrations.

While the Socializer will chat with anyone within earshot, the Relater likes to deal with a close group of confidants.

If the need for change is finally proven, Relaters want to see a plan before they'll start. Once committed, though, the Relater is like a bulldog; more than any of the other three types, he or she persists, no matter what.

THE THINKER

I'd rather be right than quick.

Thinkers probably *liked* doing term papers in school.

They're serious, analytical people with long-range goals. They cherish efficiency. They love logic. They adore accuracy.

Thinkers are the most cerebrally oriented of the four types. Like Directors, they generally prefer tasks over people. But unlike Directors, Thinkers are contemplative, cautious, and thorough—sometimes to a fault.

Thriving on details and discipline, Thinkers want clearly defined priorities and a known pace. They are natural as architects, engineers, computer programmers, and CPAs.

The key to a good life for them is making careful progress.

If Michelangelo had been a Thinker, here's how he probably would have gone about painting his famous frescoes on the ceiling of Rome's Sistine Chapel:

He'd take the project very seriously, expecting to be judged by his attention to detail. Laboriously, he would plan the complicated design, down to the proper tint on the wings of each seraphim. He'd also figure out how each scene could be painted to stand alone, lest he be stricken ill or incapacitated, or if the pope, for some reason, decided to halt the project.

Then he'd begin, doing it largely himself. He really wouldn't mind that he must spend four years alone on his back, seventy feet up in the air. That hardship would be more than made up for by the fact that this project would be: Perfect.

Would it be a masterpiece? Quite possibly. At least, that's what a Thinker would aspire to. He wouldn't expect the job to be fun, but he'd like to think that his work might be hailed for centuries as a marvel of skill, taste, and self-determination.

☑ What Excites Them? Reason

The fact-oriented Thinkers pride themselves on being meticulous. They like having correct procedures in place. They want to know in detail how things work so that they can carefully, objectively evaluate any problem.

Thinkers try to avoid embarrassment by controlling themselves and their environment. Private and proper in their personal relations, they keep their distance from huggers and touchers.

Their discipline and attention to detail can make them prodigious workers.

☑ *Greatest Asset: High-Quality Work*

Accurate, dependable, and independent, the Thinker is thorough and well organized. In fact, organization is almost as vital to Thinkers as oxygen.

One Thinker types out preaddressed labels to take on vacations so she can mail postcards to her friends more efficiently.

Thinkers study problems intently. They're good people to have on committees because they'll ask the question no one else thinks of, like, "Isn't that the same weekend as Memorial Day?"

Their follow-through is excellent.

Though a bit standoffish, they're very close to their few key friends.

☑ *Greatest Failing: Too Critical*

Thinkers can be nit-picking perfectionists. Paralysis by overanalysis can result, especially under pressure.

Few, including themselves, meet the Thinkers' high

standards. So they're often seen as demanding and picky.

Naturally conservative, they also can be overly frugal, fretting over every penny or each unrecycled soda can.

Their sense of organization can become compulsive: laying out clothes well in advance, alphabetizing items in the stockroom, or making lists of everything—including lists of their lists.

They prefer to plan everything, even spontaneity. One Thinker even makes notes about possible small-talk topics before going to office cocktail parties!

☑ Greatest Fear: Irrationality

Thinkers want clarity and order. They must finish tasks without mistakes. One of their greatest irritations is disorganized, illogical people.

Like the Relater, the Thinker is basically introverted and seeks answers by turning inward. So he or she often prefers to work with those who promote calmness or thoroughness—that is, Relaters and other Thinkers.

Once they are ready to decide an issue, human emotions are not as important as weighing all the factors and making the logical, rational, and thus most "correct," decision.

Thinkers, though they may be witty on the surface, see life's more serious, complicated sides. They can be one-person think tanks to whom no problem is too small to ponder.

They want to amass lots of facts before giving their

opinion. Thus, they are somewhat guarded, typically sharing information on a need-to-know basis and only then when they are sure it won't come back to bite them.

They *can* be hard to budge when they feel they've mastered all the facts or thought something through to its bedrock conclusion.

And they *will* make a decision, but only after having determined the specific risks, margins for error, and fall-back positions.

Having decided, they'd like nothing more than to be praised for their thoroughness.

SO . . . NOW DO YOU KNOW WHICH TYPE IS BEST?

Clearly, none of the four styles is perfect. None is *the* way. All have their advantages and disadvantages, admirers and critics.

That's fine. We need people with these different perspectives because:

- if we were all **Directors**, we'd all want to be in charge but there'd be no one to boss;
- if everybody was a **Socializer**, there'd be fun galore but we might get nothing done;
- if everyone was a **Relater**, there'd be calm and order but not much adrenaline; and
- if there were only **Thinkers**, we'd all be seen as aloof perfectionists.

Each style has its pluses and minuses. Directors excel in exerting control and making quick decisions, but they can be heavy-handed with human beings. Socializers, warm as they are in dealing with people, are sometimes disastrous with detail. A Relater lends calmness to most situations but often not much energy. And a Thinker is great at analyzing problems— sometimes where no big problems even exist.

Any of the four can get a job done. But each uses a different route to reach that goal.

Let's say, for instance, that the task is to prepare an airliner for takeoff. How do you think each of the four would handle the cockpit checklist?

Well, you can bet that a pilot who is a **Thinker** will personally focus like a laser on the most critical factors on the checklist. Then he'll use any remaining time to review the less crucial ones.

The **Director**, by contrast, probably won't want to go through the checklist personally. She'll delegate it to a junior crewmember, who'll report back in a format chosen by the Director. That way the Director can stay on top of other facets of flight preparation as well.

A pilot who is a **Socializer** would run through his checklist while chatting with his crew. He also might wait until the last moment to start the checkoff because of his usual difficulty budgeting his time.

A **Relater** would do the checklist in a machinelike manner. She'd personally go through each step—*and* in the order listed. Which is probably what the creator of the checklist had in mind.

After this introduction to the four personal styles, you probably know which one is most like you. That's important, but:

- Did you recognize other people you know?
- Did you recognize other types who rub you the wrong way?
- Did you recognize other types whom you respect and like, even though they differ from you?

Hold those thoughts! We're next going to look in more detail at where you fit in among the Big Four.

3

◆

HOW TO TELL
WHERE YOU FIT IN

You're in a rush to get to the airport, but the checkout line at the hotel is long and slow-moving. Do you:

- Take your place quietly at the end?
- Demand to see the manager?
- Ask those at the head of the line to let you in?
- Go to the end but continue to grumble and complain?

Similarly, do you slow down, or speed up, when the traffic light turns yellow? Are you the kind of person who charges right into the midst of a cocktail party, or are you more likely to linger around the edges until you see who's there and who's not?

Also, how much you talk, what risks you'll take, what kind of people irritate you, how quickly you make decisions, how readily you share your feelings, whether you're curious or competitive, analytical or accommodating—all these traits, and more, suggest your behavioral style. And that style stays with you like your fingerprints.

By now you probably have a pretty good idea of which of the four basic styles is most like you. But in the self-assessment that follows, you'll determine your style more precisely. Knowing your own style can enable you to better (1) capitalize on strengths, present and potential; and (2) reduce how often your weaknesses trip you up.

Remember, it's not uncommon to have personality traits that span more than one style. In fact, most of us aren't purely one style. We're blends, and our personal combination changes from time to time, depending on the situation and whom we're with.

Yet most of us show one primary style most of the time. That style is most evident when you're most at ease, when you're just acting like yourself, when your mind seems as if it's on automatic pilot. That's the style we'll determine here. In a later chapter, we'll refine the four basic styles more precisely and see if you're, say, a Director with strong Socializer tendencies or some other such combination.

For now, though, here's how to figure out where you likely fit among the Big Four:

THE PLATINUM RULE PERSONAL-STYLES INVENTORY

This is an informal survey, designed to determine how you *usually* act in everyday situations. The idea is to get a clear description of how you see yourself.

For each pair of statements below, distribute three points between the two alternatives (A and B), depending on how characteristic of you the statement is. Although some pairs of statements may seem equally true for you, assign more points to the alternative that is more representative of your behavior most of the time.

Examples:

- If A is very characteristic of you and B is very uncharacteristic, write "3" next to A and "0" next to B.
- If A is more characteristic of you than B, write "2" next to A and "1" next to B.
- If B is very characteristic of you and A is very uncharacteristic, write "3" next to B and "0" next to A.
- If B is more characteristic of you than A, write "2" next to B and "1" next to A.

After you have marked answers to all eighteen pairs of statements, transfer your ratings to the blanks on page 41. Please base your answers on how you *actually* behave, not on how you think you should behave. (Remember: the numbers you assign to each pair must add up to 3.)

1A_____I'm usually open to getting to know people personally and establishing relationships with them.

1B_____I'm not usually open to getting to know people personally and establishing relationships with them.

2A_____I usually react slowly and deliberately.

2B_____I usually react quickly and spontaneously.

3A_____I'm usually guarded about other people's use of my time.

3B_____I'm usually open to other people's use of my time.

4A_____I usually introduce myself at social gatherings.

4B_____I usually wait for others to introduce themselves to me at social gatherings.

5A_____I usually focus my conversations on the interests of the people involved, even if that means straying from the business or subject at hand.

5B_____I usually focus my conversations on the tasks, issues, business, or subject at hand.

6A_____I'm usually not assertive, and I can be patient with a slow pace.

6B_____I'm usually assertive, and at times I can be impatient with a slow pace.

7A_____I usually make decisions based on facts or evidence.

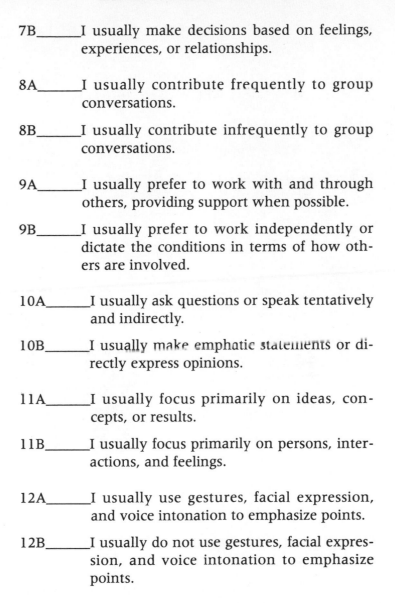

7B_____I usually make decisions based on feelings, experiences, or relationships.

8A_____I usually contribute frequently to group conversations.

8B_____I usually contribute infrequently to group conversations.

9A_____I usually prefer to work with and through others, providing support when possible.

9B_____I usually prefer to work independently or dictate the conditions in terms of how others are involved.

10A_____I usually ask questions or speak tentatively and indirectly.

10B_____I usually make emphatic statements or directly express opinions.

11A_____I usually focus primarily on ideas, concepts, or results.

11B_____I usually focus primarily on persons, interactions, and feelings.

12A_____I usually use gestures, facial expression, and voice intonation to emphasize points.

12B_____I usually do not use gestures, facial expression, and voice intonation to emphasize points.

13A_____I usually accept others' points of view (ideas, feelings, and concerns).

13B_____I usually don't accept others' points of view (ideas, feelings, and concerns).

14A_____I usually respond to risk and change in a cautious or predictable manner.

14B_____I usually respond to risk and change in a dynamic or unpredictable manner.

15A_____I usually prefer to keep personal feelings and thoughts private, sharing only when I wish to do so.

15B_____I usually find it natural and easy to share and discuss my feelings with others.

16A_____I usually seek out new or different experiences and situations.

16B_____I usually choose known or similar situations and relationships.

17A_____I'm usually responsive to others' agendas, interests, and concerns.

17B_____I'm usually directed toward my own agendas, interests, and concerns.

18A_____I usually respond to conflict slowly and indirectly.

18B_____I usually respond to conflict quickly and directly.

Please transfer your scores to the following table. (Note: Sometimes the "A" response appears first; other times, the "B" response is first.)

THE PLATINUM RULE PERSONAL-STYLES SCORING SHEET

O	G	D	I
1A	1B	2B	2A
3B	3A	4A	4B
5A	5B	6B	6A
7B	7A	8A	8B
9A	9B	10B	10A
11B	11A	12A	12B
13A	13B	14B	14A
15B	15A	16A	16B
17A	17B	18B	18A
TOTAL:	TOTAL:	TOTAL:	TOTAL:

Now, compare the O and G scores. Which is higher? Write the higher score in the blank below and circle the corresponding letter:

_____ O or G

Then compare the D and I scores. Which is higher? Write the higher score in the blank below and circle the corresponding letter:

_____ D or I

SO WHAT'S THE VERDICT?

Here's how to figure out which style is most descriptive of you—along with a quick recap of what makes that style tick.

❏ If you circled the G and the D, you tend toward being a Director.

Strengths:	Administration, taking initiative.
Weaknesses:	Impatience, insensitivity.
Irritation:	Indecision.
Goals:	Productivity, control.
Fear:	Being hustled.
Motivator:	Winning.

❏ If you circled the O and the D, you show many qualities of a Socializer:

Strengths:	Persuasion, interacting with others.
Weaknesses:	Disorganization, carelessness.
Irritation:	Routine.
Goals:	Popularity, applause.
Fear:	Loss of prestige.
Motivator:	Recognition.

❏ If you circled the O and the I, you're predominantly a Relater.

Strengths:	Servicing, listening.
Weaknesses:	Oversensitivity, indecision.
Irritation:	Insensitivity.
Goals:	Acceptance, stability.

Fear: Sudden change.
Motivator: Involvement.

❏ If you circled the G and the I, you have lots of Thinker characteristics.

Strengths: Planning, analyzing.
Weaknesses: Perfectionistic, overly critical.
Irritation: Unpredictability.
Goals: Accuracy, thoroughness.
Fear: Criticism.
Motivator: Progress.

We'll come back to your style—and the quantitative score you gave yourself—in a later chapter. Meanwhile, now that you know your own style, let's find out how to get a reading on everyone else.

4

♦

THE KEY TO GETTING
A QUICK HANDLE ON ANYBODY

You're nervously waiting outside the big glass-walled office. Soon it will be your turn. You'll be giving the new boss his initial briefing about your operation.

His predecessor was a low-key, folksy guy who liked to put his feet up on the desk, hand out cans of Diet Pepsi, and kick around the pros and cons of issues during long meetings filled with great detail and lots of personal observations. So you've carefully typed out an agenda of thirteen departmental items, some with multiple subparts, and you've thought long and hard about how you might introduce each of them in a distinctive way.

But then through the glass you see that the new boss has already brought in a bigger desk and hung lots of awards and commendations on the wall, a departure from the spartan surroundings of your former boss. And though the new manager's been on the job less than a week, he's quickly earned a reputation as a blustery, fast-talking workaholic. Now you see him pacing agitatedly, pointing his finger vigorously at another department head. Even through the glass, you can hear him haranguing about "Results, results!"

You anxiously wonder, Should I change my game plan?

The short answer: Yes. This boss is nothing like your former one. Rather than go in with your long laundry list of problems, you'd get off to a much better start with the new guy by preparing a quick executive summary and a proposed plan of attack.

Why? Well, that's what we're going to learn in this chapter: How you can turn your observations into a quick, accurate fix on anybody.

Soon you'll be able to spot Directors, Socializers, Relaters, and Thinkers as easily as you can tell a sports car from a station wagon, or a semi-trailer from a dump truck. Once you determine people's styles, you'll understand their goals, fears, motivations, how they process information, and, most important, the way they want to be treated.

In fact, by the end of this chapter you'll have the skills to get a quick reading on almost anyone. You do that by learning to read the clues. They come in three forms: verbal, vocal, and visual behavior. The verbal channel includes the words we use; or to put it another way, the *content* of our speech. The vocal and visual channels—such as voice intonation and body language—convey the *intent* of the message.

VERBAL CLUES

The simplest way to start sorting out the personality types is just to listen to people's verbal clues: How much they talk and what kinds of words and phrases they use.

Extroverts talk more. Two of our personality types— the Director and the Socializer—are outgoing, fast-paced personalities, as we've already learned. Of course they're outgoing in different ways: One's a commanding personality and the other is more of a natural showman, an entertainer.

But neither is shy. They both tend to talk a lot and do so energetically.

So, for starters, if you meet someone, especially for the first time, and they come on strong, they're likely either a Director or a Socializer. That's your first clue.

Conversely, if they're quiet and soft-spoken, they're probably a Relater or a Thinker. Those two types, more naturally introverted, are not so quick to assert themselves or reveal what they're really thinking.

So, right away, when you can peg someone as assertive and talky, or low-key and reserved, you can cut the possibilities by half. Already you're 50 percent there!

The second verbal sign is *what* people say: their words, their pace, and especially their priority.

Directors, as we've seen, are aggressive, results-oriented people for whom getting the job done and accomplishing tasks is very important. They're not shrinking violets, so you can expect them to speak quickly and strongly. They tend to listen less and talk more, usually making emphatic statements rather than asking questions.

Be alert for these kinds of statements from a Director:

"Tell him I want to talk to him ASAP."
"Let's get this settled right now."
"What's the bottom line?"
"Cut to the chase: What are the options?"
"Here's how we'll proceed. . . ."
"I want to win this battle—no ifs, ands, or buts."
"Tell me what the goal is."
"You handle it—but keep me informed."

That's a Director for you, strong and talkative, but in a way that moves the discussion firmly ahead toward his or her most prized goals: Results. Victory. Solution. Tangible Progress.

Now, the Socializer's also an outgoing, verbal person. But, as you'll recall from Chapter 2, he or she is more sociable, playful, and fun. They're more oriented toward people than tasks.

Like the Director, the Socializer is talkative—in fact, usually downright chatty—but his or her words will have a different ring. They'll be much less direct and seldom authoritarian. So the Socializer is more inclined to include you in the conversation and to be less aggressive about results.

You could expect to hear a Socializer tell more stories and jokes and say things such as:

"Hey! Here's an idea! Whattaya think?"
"Why don't you noodle on that concept for a while."
"I feel this is the way to go to . . ."
"Tell me what you think about . . ."
"Spare me the details. Just give me the drift."
"I think we're making good progress. Now let's . . ."
"My sense is that . . ."
"Let's try it a different way, just for kicks."

Again, if the person you meet is assertive and talkative, he or she is probably a Director or a Socializer. You can determine that almost instantly.

Then listen to their words. If the talk is about tasks and results—words like *output, competition, success, triumph*—it's likely a Director you're hearing. To them, life is often akin to combat, and they want to win.

A Socializer's talk will be more about people and ideas; the Socializer will use words like *feeling, impressions, team, concept,* and *ideas.* Socializers see life as more of a celebration; they don't want to triumph as much as they want to be liked and to have everyone enjoy themselves.

The Flip Side

Okay, but let's say this person you meet isn't talkative or chatty. She doesn't start off acting as if she's known you for years or as if she's been put in charge. In fact, when you meet her, she's quietly pleasant and low-key. You get a sense of a bit of a gulf separating you from her.

So, clearly, what you have here is either a Relater

or a Thinker. They both tend to be a bit quiet and introverted. They're seldom aggressive or loud. They listen more and talk less.

When they do speak, it's often with questions rather than direct statements about their own thoughts or feelings. They're the kind of people who probably wouldn't plunge into a crowded room but instead would take a few minutes to scope out the goings-on from the sidelines.

Observing that, you can eliminate Director or Socializer. But how do you distinguish between Relater and Thinker? Well, again, listen to *what* they say.

Relaters are friendly, sensitive people, maybe a bit indecisive or even acquiescent. They like to ask the opinion of others and wouldn't think of forcing their views on someone else. They like stability and being accepted. So you'll probably hear them say things like:

"I'd like to go kind of slow on this. Is that okay?"
"Have we determined the impact of this on the staff?"
"I'm not yet sure about that change."
"I really enjoy working with you."
"I'd like to help you however I can."
"We can work this out, I'm sure."
"How do you really feel about this?"
"How's this likely to end up? I'd like to know first."

Thinkers, while also reserved and slower-paced, are not as concerned with being part of the team and avoiding risk at all costs. They're very independent people. They're much more into getting things done than the Relaters but in a much more understated way than the Directors.

Thinkers are serious, precise people. If the talk at a party got around to a controversial new law just passed by Congress, Thinkers would be inclined to correct you politely if you had a fact wrong. But while they're keen on accuracy and data, they also hate to be embarrassed or make a scene. So if a conflict develops over who is right about the congressional action, they'd probably just change the subject, or get up and go talk to someone else.

Here are the kinds of phrases you might hear from a Thinker:

"Now, let's look at this logically."

"Is that really the right thing to do? Can we justify that?"

"Let's take this first step. Then we can decide step two."

"Give me all the facts first."

"What guidelines make sense for this project?"

"Precisely what do you mean?"

"I don't want any surprises."

"Have we touched all the bases?"

So, to summarize, if the person you meet is reserved and low-key, he or she is likely a Relater or a Thinker. That's a call you can make almost instantaneously.

Then listen to the person. If he's warm, friendly, and talks more about people, feelings, and togetherness, you've probably found a Relater. They see life as a team effort in which the goal is to work together amiably without making too many waves.

A Thinker, on the other hand, is also reserved but has a bit of a sharper edge. He wants to solve problems, get things done, make progress—but all in a nonobtrusive, orderly, low-key way. Thinkers see life as mainly a management problem: First, figure out the tasks, then accomplish them by methodically and carefully applying facts and logic.

Putting This into Practice

Suppose you're calling on a client for the first time. The appointment is set up by the client's secretary for 10:10 A.M. Not 10 A.M. Not "10-ish," but 10:10.

You arrive a few minutes early and are asked to take a seat in the reception area. Your client comes out of her office at 10:03, acknowledges your presence with a polite smile, and in a low voice gives a list of detailed instructions to her secretary. She then returns to her desk.

At 10:10, you're escorted into her office. She tells you where to sit, looks at her watch, and tells you that you have twenty minutes to make your presentation. You launch into your spiel.

The client, seeming interested but not enthusiastic, lets you go on at length, though again glancing at her watch. When you're done, she asks for more details about the cost, schedule, and flexibility of your proposal.

"Now, if it turns out this doesn't work for us, can we cancel after phase one without penalty?" she asks at one point. You assure her that's the case and answer some more questions. Then, as the two of you are about to close the deal, she repeats the specific points of the agreement to make sure there is no mis-understanding.

So . . . what type is she?

Well, she wasn't very chatty, so you can eliminate Director and Socializer right off the bat. A Socializer would have greeted you more warmly and would likely have gone on about the weather, your competitors, or this funny thing she saw on TV the other night. A Director wouldn't have been all that friendly but would have come on more strongly, probably taking charge of the conversation and interrupting you with pointed queries as you made your case.

So clearly we're talking about either a Relater or a Thinker. But which? Well, this client's low-key but no-nonsense approach strongly points to a Thinker. While not overly friendly, she was proper and businesslike, detail-oriented and exact. A Relater, while also low-key, would have been more personal, more interested in knowing about you and having you know more about her.

Later in this book, you'll learn how to adjust your style to work best with any of the other styles. You'll also see that many of us are combinations of the four styles. But for now, congratulations! You've learned the bare essentials of picking out each of the four types by reading their verbal clues.

Now that you know about verbal clues, perhaps you can see how in this chapter's opening anecdote, the new boss was sending out loud and clear verbal signals that he was unlike his predecessor. Whereas the former boss was a low-key, detail-oriented man (likely a Thinker), the new manager is quick-paced, assertive, and perhaps a bit blustery. His demand for "Results! Results!" should help you further peg him as a Director, a fast-paced, dominating person who's not likely to welcome patiently a detailed, point-by-point recitation of your department's issues.

VOCAL CLUES

We don't just speak words. Our voices are sophisticated instruments, and we use them to send many signals about how we're feeling and thinking.

Let's say you enter a business meeting a few moments late. You open the door, and your boss, who's chairing the meeting, says, "Look who's here!"

From these printed words, can you tell how your boss was feeling about your arrival? Annoyed? Grateful? Disgusted? Or happy?

No, you can't tell. You need more information. Information you can only get through such voice intonations as speed, inflection, pitch, resonance, rhythm, and volume. These vocal clues are not about what's said or how much is said—but *how* it's said.

Each of the four behavioral styles has a range of vocal characteristics. Directors and Socializers are confident, outgoing people. So they speak quickly and with confident-sounding intonations.

Directors, especially, communicate forcefully and with an intonation that often seems to carry an implicit challenge. When you talk to a Director, you often sense that he or she is talking down to you, or barely tolerating you. They don't actually say that. But that's sometimes the unspoken signal their voice emits.

Socializers, good storytellers that they are, have the most variety in vocal quality of any of the four styles. So they use lots of inflection, and as they share their personal feelings, they greatly vary the pitch of their speech. A bit dramatic, they may speak rapidly and often loudly. "Look at me! I'm something special" is the unspoken message you often hear.

Relaters and Thinkers, on the other hand, usually speak slowly and often come across as more contemplative, and perhaps less confident. Relaters normally use a steady, even-tempered delivery. They often project warmth and sincerity into their voices. They silently announce, "I'm a friendly person—but I'm neither pushy nor do I like to be pushed."

The Thinkers typically use the least inflection of any of the four, often speaking in something of a monotone, calm, measured, and with few variations in pitch. Their voice doesn't tell you much about what they're thinking. You sense that they're "neutral," trying neither to charm you nor to control you.

VISUAL CLUES

There's one other obvious external indicator of style: body language. This can take many forms. For instance, facial expressions, or the lack of them. Hand and body movements, such as touching, pointing, and gesturing. Eye contact, whether steady or intermittent. And even spontaneous, dramatic actions, like leaping up from a chair or giving someone a hearty slap on the back.

Not surprisingly, Directors and Socializers again come across as emphatic, assertive people who make strong first impressions—good or bad. Physically, too, they take the initiative.

From Directors you'd expect a firm handshake, steady eye contact, and frequent gestures—often a jabbing, stabbing motion as they speak—to back up their strong statements. Their body language, like everything else about them, is fast-moving and frequently suggests impatience and power.

Similarly, the Socializer employs a lot of hand and body movement while speaking and is typically the most facially animated of the four. Big smiles, furrowed brows, cants of the head, and quizzical looks come to them as naturally as breathing. The Socializer also is the most inclined toward spontaneous touching—a reassuring hand on the shoulder, a fond pat on the back, a big, two-handed handshake.

Eye contact by Relaters is intermittent. Sometimes they'll even look at the floor rather than directly at you. Handshakes are more tentative and gentle, and their slower-moving body language suggests calmness and patience.

"Poker-faced" is a phrase probably first coined about a Thinker because they make few facial expressions or gestures. Further, because they have a strong sense of space, they're not inclined toward touching.

So now let's take a look at how we might interpret the vocal, verbal, and visual clues in a work situation.

WHO'S WHO AT THE SEMINAR?

You're giving a sales seminar that's set for 8:30 A.M. after an 8 o'clock coffee-and-doughnuts session. You arrive about 7:50 and find Ann already there, pad and pencils neatly laid out on the table in front of her.

She stands, and the two of you shake hands. She manages a minimal smile. You ask a few questions about her and her job, and you receive short, polite answers, but little small talk. You notice that she stands some distance from you.

A few other seminar participants arrive and find their way to the coffee and doughnuts. Then at about 8:15, Bob steps hesitantly into the doorway and softly asks, "Excuse me. Is this the training seminar for the sales department?"

When told that it is, he breathes a sigh, walks in, pours himself some coffee, and mentions how he's been looking forward to this presentation for a long time. It'll be helpful, he says, both for work and at home. Bob asks you some more questions, listening intently to your answers. He says he hopes there's not too much role-playing in front of the group.

About that time, Charley strides in. "Hey, is this the sales seminar? Or is everybody here because there's free coffee?" he asks with a laugh.

Before you can reply, he pours himself some, admits he can't function "without my black poison," and jumps into the conversation about the role-playing. "Actually, I kind of like that," he says, before telling how he managed to embarrass himself at the last seminar by impersonating the big boss just as the boss walked past the open door to the conference room.

Then the last participant, Deborah, appears. She walks briskly into the room, takes a seat close to the front, and says to you, "I'm scheduled to be somewhere else by ten-thirty. Will you be done by then? If not, can this class be repeated next month so those of us who can't stay will have another chance to sit in? There are plenty who aren't here, so rescheduling may be necessary in any case."

Judging by the verbal, vocal, and visual clues, what's the style of Ann, the first person described? Bob? Charley? And Deborah, the last one?

Ann appears to be a classic Thinker. She shows a disinterest in small talk, a lack of facial animation, restrained gestures, and generally self-contained behavior.

Bob, on the other hand, volunteered information about his personal feelings and with his sigh and his earnestness, showed himself to be relatively open, yet with the hesitation and soft voice that suggests a Relater.

Charley, the talkative fellow who headed straight for the coffee amid a stream of stories and self-admissions, seems to be a Socializer. He likes being the center of attention. His speech was rapid, his movements were quick, and his gestures and animation were obvious.

And last, there was Deborah, who strode in as if she had called the meeting. Her behavior suggests that she's a Director. Strong, sure, and in command, she spoke very confidently. Although only a rank-and-file attendee, she sought to influence the agenda.

Verbal, vocal, and visual clues are key to getting a

handle on anyone's behavioral style. To make style identification even simpler, we've combined these clues in a unique way to form The Platinum Grid.

THE PLATINUM GRID

Directors and Socializers are often grouped together, as are Relaters and Thinkers, because of some basic similarities:

DIRECTORS/SOCIALIZERS	RELATERS/THINKERS
Talkative	Quiet
Animated	Restrained
Fast-paced	Slow-paced

But, as you may have noted by now, it's not quite that simple. Beyond those most obvious parallels, there are other connections. The quiet Relaters and the assertive Socializers, for example, both are people-oriented. The brash Directors and the introverted Thinkers both give a high priority to tasks.

To pick up on those differences, we use a slightly more sophisticated technique called The Platinum Grid. It's a linchpin of learning to identify and adapt to personal styles.

Like the use of verbal, vocal, and visual clues, The Platinum Grid helps you place a person in one of the four basic behavioral styles. But it picks up on more subtle variations in behavior among the styles, and thus may be more accurate.

Using this method, you start out by first noting this behavior:

- *Direct/Indirect:*   the amount of involvement a person uses to influence people and situations

Direct people are "forward"—they approach risk, decisions, and change in a quick, spontaneous way. They're frequent, strong contributors to group conversations. They often make emphatic statements and express their opinions readily. They can be confronting, intense, assertive.

A direct person might say, "Tell Jones I want to talk to him ASAP!" An indirect person, on the other hand, is more likely to ask Jones's secretary to have him come to the office when it's convenient.

Direct people are bolder, like batters who don't keep track of the strikeouts, only the home runs. To them, the *number* of successes is more important than the *percentage* of success. So they swing for the fences, disdaining singles and doubles.

They also aren't afraid to break or bend the established rules in order to get results. Their motto might be: "It's easier to beg forgiveness later than to seek permission first."

They're less patient, and more competitive. When things go wrong, they don't take it personally. Instead, seeing the source of the problem as the "system" or more timid souls, they redouble their efforts.

Indirect people, on the other hand, are more easygoing and show better self-control. They approach risk, decision, or change slowly and cautiously. They like to know the plan fully before committing, and even then they may want an escape hatch. They're understated: They reserve their opinion and are more patient and diplomatic. They tend to follow the rules.

They approach life defensively, often seeking ways to prevent failure rather than achieve a smashing success. They bet on sure winners, and they like the high success ratios that such a strategy brings. When there is a mistake, they're likely to look for a personal flaw that caused the failure. "How could I have been so stupid?" they'll ask themselves after a setback.

Socially speaking, they prefer to wear both belt and suspenders. They'd probably linger on the fringes of a crowd before plunging in. They're not interested in drawing attention to themselves.

So here's how direct and indirect people match up:

Direct	Indirect
Takes risks	Avoids risk
Swift decisions	Slower to decide
Confronting, expressive	Less assertive
Impatient	Easygoing, patient
Talks and tells	Listens and asks
Outgoing	Reserved
Offers opinions freely	Keeps opinions private

Now let's make directness versus indirectness one leg of a chart, like so:

Direct—————————————————————Indirect

The other major dimension of The Platinum Grid is:

- *Open/Guarded:*   Describes his or her inner thoughts, feelings, and motives

Open people are emotionally available. They're the kind who are commonly described by others as relaxed, warm, responsive, informal, "nice," or "sweet." They crave enjoyable conversation. So they're the kind who would be more willing to listen, or contribute, to a long, drawn-out story about cranky old Uncle Jess's run-in with the nurses at the convalescent home.

Open people are personable and give the top priority to people, not tasks. Being relationship-oriented, they're quick to share personal feelings. Open people are more flexible about their time, welcoming digressions more than guarded people do.

They also tend to base their decisions more upon intuition than hard facts or data. People who are open use their bodies and facial expressions a lot when they talk, and they often talk more about feelings than facts.

Guarded people, on the other hand, keep their distance, both physically and emotionally. They are often viewed by others as a bit formal or proper, hiding their personal feelings from people they don't know very well. They favor facts and detail over emotions and are less likely to use body language or to change expression when speaking.

People often say about a guarded person, "He's not easy to get to know. But once you do, he's a great guy!" Guarded folks are more disciplined about their time and try to keep conversations focused on the issues at hand.

They place a high priority on getting things done, and they like structure: They want to know the rules, the plan, the outline, rather than just "winging it."

So here are the contrasting traits:

Open	Guarded
Relaxed, warm	Formal, proper
Likes opinions	Favors facts
Relationship-oriented	Task-oriented
Readily shares feelings	Keeps feelings private
Flexible about time	Disciplined about time
Feeling-oriented	Thinking-oriented
Spontaneous	Prefers planning

When we plot the open/guarded trait on our graph, superimposing it over the indirect/direct axis, the two dimensions quickly reveal the four personality types:

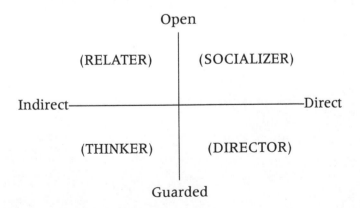

63

TWO KEY QUESTIONS

So this is another quick way of accurately determining anyone's personal style. Just answer two questions: Is the person more direct or indirect? Is he or she more open or guarded?

Let's say you set up a luncheon meeting with a new client. He greets you warmly at the restaurant, asks the waiter to give the two of you some time to chat, and readily tells you his experiences with certain dishes on the menu before going on to speak at length about his business.

Even at this early stage, you're picking up clues. So you mentally go through your checklist. It looks something like this:

Open	*Guarded*
Relaxed, warm	Formal, proper
Likes opinions	Favors facts
Relationship-oriented	Task-oriented
Readily shares feelings	Keeps feelings private
Flexible about time	Disciplined about time
Feeling-oriented	Thinking-oriented
Spontaneous	Prefers planning

You think to yourself, I'm observing a man with higher-than-average openness. He's definitely not guarded. So, clearly, he's going to be somewhere at the top of the chart, meaning that you can automatically eliminate the two guarded styles (Thinker and Director).

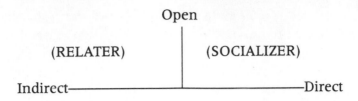

So he's either a Relater or a Socializer, both warm, open types. The question then becomes, Which is he, direct or indirect?

You observe him further. He proudly—almost boastfully—tells you all about himself and his company and why it's head-and-shoulders above its competition. He periodically tosses in a question about your business or your family. Twice he calls the waiter over to the table, once to ask for more bread and then for refills of iced tea. So although he's friendly, he's also intense and assertive. And not too patient.

So you try to pin him down by reviewing the direct and indirect traits. You come up with something like this:

Direct	*Indirect*
Takes risks	Avoids risks
Swift decisions	Cautious decisions
Confronting, expressive	Less assertive
Impatient	Easygoing, patient
Talks and tells	Listens and asks
Outgoing	Reserved
Offers opinions freely	Keeps opinions private

You easily conclude that he's direct. So you can eliminate the remaining indirect style, the Relater.

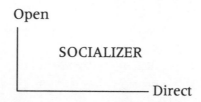

Open

SOCIALIZER

Direct

Voilà! By process of elimination, you conclude that this open and direct person is probably a Socializer.

BACK TO THE NEW BOSS

Now, remember the example that began this chapter? You were outside the glass-walled office anxiously watching and listening to your new boss and wondering how to handle him.

Even though you haven't spoken to him yet, several things should be clear now that you're a trained observer. He's assertive; he speaks loudly and rapidly. He seems impatient and appears to do most of the talking. He's expressive and confrontative.

So he must be . . . direct.

But he's also demonstrative about wanting "Results!" He's put plaques and commendations on his wall, suggesting an emphasis on accomplishment. His bigger desk hints at greater formality. His fast-paced, outgoing style emphasizes tasks more than feelings.

So he's . . . guarded.

Put the two together: He's direct and guarded. He's likely a Director.

That's why he's not going to want to listen to a long list of details from you. That's why you'll do much better with him if you come in with a quick summary of problems and a plan of action he can review.

Don't try to charm him with a pun-filled joke you heard on the golf course or that amusing tale of your four-year-old's attempt to bathe the family mutt. Don't think your winning smile or your how-much-this-company-means-to-me speech will cut any ice.

Instead, give the new boss facts, plans, a promise of progress. Then deliver.

That's what he's looking for. And you understand that already, without even having spoken to him. That's because you know and practice **The Platinum Rule**.

5

♦

HOW TO READ
THE MIXED STYLES

By now you've got a pretty good sense of where you fit in among the four basic behavioral styles. But are you pure? Do you seem to be, say, a total Socializer? An unwavering Director? A never-to-be-moved Thinker, or a Relater who wouldn't dream of ever thinking or acting for just a moment like any of the other three?

Probably not. You likely see some traits in the other three styles that also could describe you on occasion. Actually, only about 20 percent of those tested fall solely within a single style. The rest of us are combinations of the styles. And those combinations can be pinpointed to define more precisely how you're likely to act and how you're usually perceived.

Think of the range of styles as being a lot like a painter's palette. We all know the color blue, for example, and we all know that it can be as diverse as indigo and robin's-egg, cerulean and cobalt. Yet we recognize each of those shades as being blue.

Likewise, most of us are a blend of personal styles, yet retain the recognizable characteristics of a Director, Socializer, Relater, or Thinker. Many of us have some of each behavioral style in his or her makeup. And some situations or roles bring out certain of those traits.

For example, Socializers, as we saw in the last chapter, are very open as well as quite direct. But *how* open and how direct can vary. Those who tilt toward being very open and somewhat direct might be called Relating Socializers. By contrast, a Socializer who is less open and less direct may best be described as a Thinking Socializer.

RECOGNIZABLE SUBSTYLES

In this chapter, we'll show how to read the sixteen possible mixed styles, or substyles, which result from the most common combinations. You may be able to pinpoint the substyles of friends or associates on this sixteen-style grid. But if so, that's a side benefit. This chapter's really for *you*, for your enjoyment and your growth.

Find *your* substyle, and we'll give you a thumbnail sketch. We'll show you what sets your substyle apart, what motivates you, and how to work better with tasks and with people. We'll also suggest some specific Personal Empowerment Pointers for increasing your effectiveness.

Each of the four basic styles contains three additional substyles. This is easy to conceptualize when you look at the following graph.

Open

Relating RELATER	Socializing RELATER	Relating SOCIALIZER	Socializing SOCIALIZER
Thinking RELATER	Directing RELATER	Thinking SOCIALIZER	Directing SOCIALIZER
Relating THINKER	Socializing THINKER	Relating DIRECTOR	Socializing DIRECTOR
Thinking THINKER	Directing THINKER	Thinking DIRECTOR	Directing DIRECTOR

Indirect ... **Direct**

Vertical scale (top to bottom): 27 26 25 24 23 22 21 20 19 18 17 16 15 14 | 14 15 16 17 18 19 20 21 22 23 24 25 26 27

Horizontal scale: 27 26 25 24 23 22 21 20 19 18 17 16 15 14 — 14 15 16 17 18 19 20 21 22 23 24 25 26 27

Guarded

To find out where you fit among these mixed styles, please go back to the Scoring Sheet on page 41 and look at your score on the self-assessment. You should have two sets of letter/number combinations.

The first dimension is that of "O" or "G," or for "Open" or "Guarded." The second dimension is "D" or "I," standing for "Direct" or "Indirect."

Please plot your scores on the graph above, using the two dimensions you indicated as highest on the Scoring Sheet.

If you circled the "O" on your Scoring Sheet, plot its number on the upper-half of the vertical line. If you circled the "G" on your Scoring Sheet, plot its number on the lower-half of the vertical line. If you circled the "I" on your Scoring Sheet, plot its number on the left-half of the horizontal line. If you circled the "D" on your Scoring Sheet, plot its number on the right-half of the horizontal line. Where the two scores intersect is the substyle that you've said best describes your tendencies.

For example, if your scores on your Scoring Sheet were 24 "O" and 26 "D," your substyle would be Socializing Socializer.

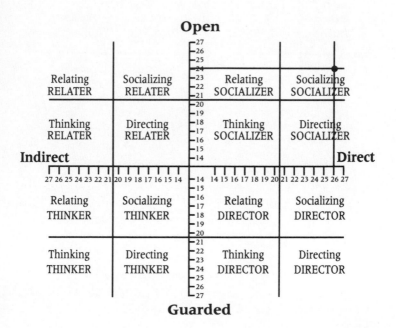

Open

Relating RELATER	Socializing RELATER	Relating SOCIALIZER	Socializing SOCIALIZER
Thinking RELATER	Directing RELATER	Thinking SOCIALIZER	Directing SOCIALIZER
Relating THINKER	Socializing THINKER	Relating DIRECTOR	Socializing DIRECTOR
Thinking THINKER	Directing THINKER	Thinking DIRECTOR	Directing DIRECTOR

Indirect ... **Direct**

Guarded

Open

Relating RELATER	Socializing RELATER	Relating SOCIALIZER	Socializing SOCIALIZER
Thinking RELATER	Directing RELATER	Thinking SOCIALIZER	Directing SOCIALIZER
Relating THINKER	Socializing THINKER	Relating DIRECTOR	Socializing DIRECTOR
Thinking THINKER	Directing THINKER	Thinking DIRECTOR	Directing DIRECTOR

Indirect

27 26 25 24 23 22 21 20 19 18 17 16 15 14 — 14 — 15 16 17 18 19 20 21 22 23 24 25 26 27

Direct

27 26 25 24 23 22 21 20 19 18 17 16 15 14

14 15 16 17 18 19 20 21 22 23 24 25 26 27

Guarded

If your scores on your Scoring Sheet were 15 "G" and 22 "I," your substyle would be Relating Thinker.

Open

		27 26 25 24 23 22 21		
Relating RELATER	Socializing RELATER		Relating SOCIALIZER	Socializing SOCIALIZER
Thinking RELATER	Directing RELATER	20 19 18 17 16 15 14	Thinking SOCIALIZER	Directing SOCIALIZER

Indirect   **Direct**

27 26 25 24 23 22 21 20 19 18 17 16 15 14   14   14 15 16 17 18 19 20 21 22 23 24 25 26 27

		15 16 17 18 19 20		
Relating THINKER	Socializing THINKER		Relating DIRECTOR	Socializing DIRECTOR
Thinking THINKER	Directing THINKER	21 22 23 24 25 26 27	Thinking DIRECTOR	Directing DIRECTOR

Guarded

If your scores on your Scoring Sheet were 24 "G" and 17 "D," your substyle would be Thinking Director.

IMPLICATIONS OF YOUR SUBSTYLE

Bear in mind that this assessment is based on your *perception*, so it's subject to bias. But it still should offer a great deal of insight and food for thought.

In the pages that follow, we'll briefly look at each of those sixteen possibilities. But first, a few words about the implications of your substyle score.

- You may find a surprising number of assets. But before your ego gets too inflated, read on: You'll likely also discover more weaknesses—or "growth opportunities"—than you imagined.
- Be happy and accepting of who you are. It's not uncommon to wish you were more like someone else. We all aspire to be "better." But the key to success is *to improve who you are* rather than trying to become someone else.
- Your personal style has developed for just one purpose: to serve your unique needs and wants. You're the product of your own experiences and influences—such as your parents, upbringing, education, successes, and failures. All of these have affected your priorities, including how you see and react to situations.
- What's the "best" style? That's like asking what's the best color, or the best food, or the best kind of terrain. Each has its own worth, and each is a rich part of life's mosaic.

Now let's look at those sixteen substyles.

THE DIRECTING DIRECTOR

("The Commander")

If you're a Directing Director, you're motivated by new opportunities, by the thrill of "the chase." You speak your mind, and you take risks. You're often happy as a serial entrepreneur who's driven to pursue his or her own ideas and interests.

You have a fierce desire to be number one. Once you've triumphed, though, you may quickly move on to new conquests, as, for example, do many CEOs who move from company to company trying to resuscitate those firms.

Your theme song could be, "I Did It My Way," sung, of course, by Frank Sinatra, another Director.

Your tendencies include these:

- wanting to have the final say, to be the conqueror;
- disliking inaction, predictability, and lack of change;
- thinking your way is the only way;
- taking on new challenges;
- wanting to pursue your own path;
- taking charge of situations; and
- deciding things yourself whether others agree or not.

Your Growth Opportunities

With tasks: When distressed, you may stop listening and can become dictatorial. But instead of trying to bludgeon people and organizations through your personal power, you might work to develop more of a team approach. Share some praise and show that you value the contributions of others. That will get you more and better results—especially when you aren't around to crack the whip.

With people: You can help yourself by controlling your need to control. Doing so will help you appear strong, sensible, and reasonable instead of hostile, domineering, or stubborn. In addition, seek to become better at coaching or counseling by taking the time to listen to people's feelings or problems. It can improve your performance *and* theirs.

Personal Empowerment Pointers

- Praise others genuinely, directly, and more often.
- Become a better coach and counselor by providing people with the time and sincere interest they need.
- Back off when you sense that your need for control is limiting the motivation and contributions of others.

THE SOCIALIZING DIRECTOR

("The Adventurer")

You're propelled by a desire for control and independence. So while you see people as a primary means for achieving dominance, you're also wary of those who may take advantage of you or beat you to a goal.

You may find yourself surrounded by followers who are attracted to your charisma. And while you like that, you like *results* even more.

Your tendencies include these:

- being tenacious;
- standing up for yourself;
- seeking to get things done quickly;
- expressing confidence in your ability to achieve and make things happen;
- downplaying your mistakes and weaknesses while focusing on successes and strengths;
- cutting corners to reach your goals more quickly and efficiently; and
- becoming forceful and less team-oriented under pressure.

Your Growth Opportunities

With tasks: You're often impatient when dealing with complex situations or long-term projects. When pressured, you have a tendency to force-fit solutions. You can benefit by learning to pay attention to available information as well as people's feelings.

With people: Socializing Directors have fast lifestyles and are driven to achieve. You should relax! It will help fulfill you, restore your energy, and improve the quality not only of your life but of the lives of those around you.

Personal Empowerment Pointers

- Take the time to ask others about their expectations, concerns, and efforts.
- Sort tasks into "Critical" and "Less Critical" categories. Then divide "Critical" ones into "Urgent" (requiring immediate action *if* the task is to be accomplished), "Short-term" (requiring action in the next one to three months), and "Long-term" (requiring action within six to twelve months).
- Focus first on what results you can't live without. Then take on those tasks where you *must* see significant improvement, and later those where you'd *like* to see improvements.

THE RELATING DIRECTOR

("The Producer")

You're an industrious go-getter who focuses on goals and proceeds full speed ahead. But you're willing to be supportive of others if it will help achieve your objectives.

You place a great deal of importance on completing tasks from start to finish, preferably by yourself. In fact, Relating Directors often seem in constant motion, totally engrossed in their projects.

Your tendencies include these:

- disliking being told what to do, or when or how to do something;
- being reluctant to change what you think or how you feel;
- delegating tasks only if absolutely necessary;
- acting competitively, especially when pushing yourself to new levels or in new directions;
- making sure that production is completed on schedule;
- depending on plans for action and follow-up routines; and
- becoming tenacious and focused when under pressure.

Your Growth Opportunities

With tasks: You're so highly focused that you can benefit by broadening your perspective. Learn to be effective outside your comfort zone by considering different points of view and other ways to achieve goals. Because you're often too "either-or" in your decision-making, practicing flexibility would help you to solve problems more creatively.

With people: Show confidence in others by delegating and giving people tasks that will be fulfilling for them. You also can benefit by creating more free time and space in your life as well as generally appreciating and tolerating differences among people.

Personal Empowerment Pointers

- Ask others to share their ideas on how to accomplish tasks and on how to satisfy their expectations and yours.
- When making or implementing decisions, check with at least three to five other knowledgeable people to see if there's a consensus. If you don't find a pattern, widen the search.
- Be more genuinely open with others by revealing your real feelings and addressing theirs.

THE THINKING DIRECTOR

("The Pioneer")

Thinking Directors are future-oriented people who often become bored with day-to-day, routine details. Their goals and standards are generally more rigorous than those of most people. Thus, you can be quite self-critical—even unrealistically demanding of yourself.

Your tendencies include these:

- wanting to change the way things are done;
- performing to your own standards;
- seeking control over people, situations, and procedures;
- not expressing your innermost thoughts and feelings;
- striving to accomplish the unusual;
- fearing you won't meet your self-imposed requirements; and
- becoming demanding and even more detached under pressure.

Your Growth Opportunities

With tasks: Your very high expectations mean you often end up being too hard on yourself. This can be self-defeating; you can spend too much time thinking negatively.

You'd benefit by developing collaborative problem-solving and people-management skills. Enlightened Thinking Directors have learned to empower not just themselves but others.

With people: Thinking Directors have twice the tendency to be task-oriented—from their Thinker side and from their Director side. As a result, they're so focused on work that they can appear aloof or calculating. But by showing more genuine warmth and interest in people, you can multiply your effectiveness.

Personal Empowerment Pointers

- Be more realistic in what you expect of yourself and others. First, focus on what's working well; next, what's getting better; and finally, what else can be done now to make further progress. This attitudinal shift works best when first applied to yourself and then related to others.
- Take training in—or learn from mentors or colleagues—how to enlist the creative potential or unused talent of others.
- Minimize your tendency to be aloof and guarded. This can include such simple adjustments as smiling more, asking others how they feel about things, giving approving head nods, or making comments such as "That's really interesting," "I can see your point," and "That's quite helpful."

THE SOCIALIZING SOCIALIZER

("The Entertainer")

You like being friendly and fun to be with. Being viewed as the life of the party energizes you, and if there is no party, you may create one.

You are not, to put it mildly, a loner. Your motto: "Never waste a crowd." Your theme: "The good life is a good time all the time."

You need recognition. How much you get shapes your emotional highs and lows. Without that recognition, you lose interest and energy, and then your effort and output can nose-dive.

You are very receptive to change. And as an advocate for change, you infuse others with enthusiasm and optimism.

In addition, you're a quick decision-maker and naturally possess what social psychologists have identified as the single most valuable asset in dealing with people: personal warmth.

Your tendencies include these:

- seeking approval and being motivated by acceptance;
- praising people;
- being exuberant, emotional, outgoing, and optimistic;
- giving free rein to your emotions;
- being very liberal with your use of time;
- overlooking physical, emotional, political, and philosophical differences;

- starting a lot of activities but finishing few of them completely; and
- becoming sentimental and even careless under pressure.

Your Growth Opportunities

With tasks: Because you're interested in so many things, you may have a shorter attention span than people with the other styles. So you often avoid extensive detail or follow-through. You're easily bored by routines and complexities that take you away from people, or cause difficulties with them.

So it's important to try to improve your attention to key details and to follow through on commitments. Start by using checklists and calendars. Make a deliberate effort to sustain interest on projects, even ones that don't excite you.

With people: Socializing Socializers avoid conflicts at all costs. That's because confrontations pose the possibility of loss of recognition and approval. But this can also happen if friction isn't realistically addressed. So you need to get better at listening and managing conflict. You also may benefit by avoiding getting too deeply involved with people too quickly, thus minimizing entanglements you might later regret.

- Make use of daily planners, calendars, checklists, and other proven, practical tools for becoming better organized.
- Be more cautious about moving too quickly or overpromising before jumping into relationships.
- Develop the serious, nonentertaining side of your personality by studying how to improve your skills in analytical listening, conflict resolution, and decision-making.

THE DIRECTING SOCIALIZER

("The Enthusiast")

You're exuberant, bubbly, and well spoken. Your warmth and charisma are natural magnets that attract others. You're so persuasive that you could sell eggs to a hen.

Prestige is important to you, and so you seek status symbols. You're also good at cultivating contacts and have a network of people you can call on for virtually anything.

Directing Socializers love being a spokesperson or presenter of new ideas, grand initiatives, and noteworthy projects that spur people by emotionally appealing to their hopes, dreams, and fascinations.

Your tendencies include these:

- seeking and enjoying status symbols;
- admiring people who express themselves well;
- disliking routines, slow paces, and needless details;
- being comfortable delegating as well as taking charge;
- exuding a positive, enthusiastic outlook on life;
- being persuasive and inspirational;
- trusting other people quickly and giving them a lot of latitude; and
- becoming soft or evasive when under pressure.

Your Growth Opportunities

With tasks: You focus on the big picture and keep moving from one new opportunity to the next. As a result, you may not fully understand what's involved in accomplishing difficult or complex tasks.

You can significantly strengthen your performance by: (a) showing more commitment and follow-through on key tasks; (b) trying to be a more analytical thinker and listener; and (c) staying current with changing know-how.

With people: Try to be less impulsive, especially when a low-keyed approach is more appropriate, such as during conflict or negotiations. You can also help yourself by working more closely with people who are task-oriented.

PERSONAL EMPOWERMENT POINTERS

- Improve your ability to deal with the substance of tasks by targeted reading, training, and asking for the help of mentors or colleagues.
- State your positive views and intentions in more low-keyed ways while providing plenty of opportunity for others to express themselves.
- Make it a point to learn from Relaters how to focus better on routine, from Thinkers how to be efficient with tasks, and from Directors about efficiency with people, including dealing directly with resistance.

THE RELATING SOCIALIZER

("The Helper")

You're a low-key and inclusive person who makes others feel comfortable and wanted. In fact, you fit into one of the two most naturally supportive styles.

You're a natural conversationalist who both listens and expresses yourself with ease. You seek positive relationships and enjoy being involved with many different people in many different situations—in fact, the more, the merrier.

Relating Socializers are esteem builders, cheerleaders. In conflict, though, they often lack thick skins and assertiveness.

Your tendencies include these:

- empathizing and projecting genuine concern;
- becoming overly subjective about people you care about;
- avoiding conflict and tension with others;
- being dependable, caring, and responsible;
- listening to people's feelings and sharing your own;
- showing confidence and trust in people;
- preferring people-oriented, positive work environments; and
- becoming too submissive or unrealistic under pressure.

Your Growth Opportunities

With tasks: You'd benefit by learning when and how to take charge of a situation. You may procrastinate by waiting for others to provide direction. In highly competitive situations, such as sales, you would benefit by seeking coaching on assertiveness.

With people: Being half-Relater, half-Socializer, you have strong people needs. Because you have an extraordinary desire to please people, you can become exhausted by their demands. So you need to learn to say no sometimes.

You also have difficulty dealing with conflict because when people express displeasure or disagreement, you interpret it as personal rejection. You need to learn to deal with the reality of conflict rather than avoiding it.

PERSONAL EMPOWERMENT POINTERS

- Be more assertive about *your* personal needs—including preserving your energy and meeting your goals.
- Learn conflict-resolution and negotiating skills.
- Get training or coaching in how to set priorities, manage resources, and monitor tasks.

THE THINKING SOCIALIZER

("The Impresser")

You're a people-oriented thinker with high expectations for yourself and others. You like to make good impressions. In fact, for the Thinking Socializer, style is often as important as content.

You show an admirable balance between thinking and feeling, and thus you can be analytical as well as intuitive about people.

Your tendencies include these:

- wanting to achieve results with flair;
- seeing winning as an all-or-nothing proposition;
- judging people by their ability to make things happen;
- working harder when bigger risks or rewards are at stake;
- preferring to share in work and goals with people;
- being concerned about looking bad;

- wanting to do things the "best" way; and
- becoming restless, short-tempered, and even lashing out when under pressure.

Your Growth Opportunities

With tasks: You tend to underestimate the time and effort required by you or others to accomplish tasks. So you should pace yourself better and draw on outside resources. Be more selective about the tasks you take on and don't hesitate to ask others to do their parts.

With people: Your hard-driving approach means you tend to be impatient, especially when stressed or under the gun. If you blow off steam, you may later regret what was said or done because of its impact on your image. So learning to relax and to enjoy regular recreation is important for recharging your battery.

Personal Empowerment Pointers

- Pace yourself better by adding one-third to one-half the time to original estimates of when tasks can be done. Similarly, reduce by one-third to one-half the number of projects you take on.
- Maintain your perspective by seeking to be less emotional and intense about noncritical situations.
- Take a stress-management course and learn simple breathing exercises as a way to deal with pressure.

THE RELATING RELATER

("The Servicer")

You're easy to approach, like to get along with people, and are mild-mannered and modest. You're most comfortable with noncontroversial positions that don't attract attention or ruffle feathers. You prefer situations where you can be of service to people.

Like the proverbial tortoise, you realize there's a lot more to winning a race than speed. Thus, you're methodical and prefer proven procedures that are followed calmly, step-by-step.

Your tendencies include these:

- wanting acceptance and involvement when working with others;
- being reserved and supportive;
- fearing a loss of stability springing from confusing changes or personal strife;
- following established procedures and proven practices;
- following tasks through to completion;
- being concrete, specific, and practical;
- preferring to complete a limited number of tangible, identifiable tasks in a comfortable period of time; and
- becoming submissive when under pressure.

Your Growth Opportunities

With tasks: You can benefit by learning to deal better with change and stress. You may need to come to grips with the reality of fluctuating workloads, quick turnaround times, and limited resources. That means controlling your tendency to be slow moving and indecisive. This is especially true if you're in a management or leadership position.

With people: Because you have a need to please others, you too often tell them only what they want to hear. Such placating can undermine relationships. You also may need to work on being more assertive.

Personal Empowerment Pointers

- Get training in collaborative problem-solving and conflict resolution. Apply these new skills, first, in lower-risk situations with people with whom you already have a good relationship.
- Be more forthright in expressing your views.
- Ask others for ideas and support as you seek to become more decisive and independent and to take more risks.

THE DIRECTING RELATER

("The Go-Getter")

You're identified by your busy, industrious approach to tasks. Constantly active at work or at play, you're driven and goal-oriented. With great energy, you set schedules, ensure that deadlines are met, and take a disciplined, step-by-step approach to getting things done.

Your tendencies include these:

- enjoying being industrious;
- taking charge of tasks;
- eagerly and competitively diving into your work;
- breaking tasks down into parts and supervising closely those parts being done by others;
- being less comfortable with complex or multiple tasks;
- looking for concrete, short-term results, especially if they bring personal rewards or recognition; and
- becoming rigid and guarded when under pressure.

Your Growth Opportunities

With tasks: Directing Relaters can benefit by understanding more of the big picture. Make sure you are clear about a project before jumping in with your full energy. Retain the support of people who'll be involved or affected by the work.

With people: While you like to do things yourself, you must learn to delegate more. You have a tendency to spread yourself too thin, so limit your involvement in less critical tasks.

Personal Empowerment Pointers

- Make sure you understand the overall goal and context before you jump headfirst into a task.
- Ask others to share their ideas on how to accomplish tasks and how to satisfy their expectations and yours.
- When making or implementing decisions, check with at least three to five other knowledgeable people to see if there's a consensus. If you don't find a pattern, widen the search.

THE SOCIALIZING RELATER

("The Harmonizer")

You belong to one of the most accepting of all the personality styles. You enjoy being around people but prefer the focus to be on others. You have a naturally warm disposition, and people are comfortable opening up to you.

So you're adept at starting and sustaining harmonious relationships. You're tolerant, understanding, supportive, and a natural listener.

Your tendencies include these:

- projecting a warm, caring attitude and preferring the same from others;
- enjoying displays of affection and approval;
- disliking aggression and conflict;
- serving as a sounding board for people;
- being turned off by confusion or complexity;
- overdoing helpfulness, empathy, or sympathy; and
- becoming more expressive or emotional under pressure.

Your Growth Opportunities

With tasks: Because you're so people-oriented, your growth opportunities are mostly with tasks. You especially should work to strengthen your problem-solving and decision-making skills. Those skills can help you better deal with complex, unwieldy tasks.

With people: You're so good at building relationships that there's little room for improvement here. But you should monitor the balance between pleasing yourself and pleasing others. That's because you sometimes spend so much energy on others that you can neglect your own needs.

Personal Empowerment Pointers

- Try to be more fast-paced when dealing with Directors and Socializers and in situations where there's time pressure or other tension.

- Take training in problem-solving and decision-making, or find a mentor or coach who can help you.
- Think about what personally satisfies *you*, independent of the pleasure you get from helping others. Then try to meet those separate needs as well.

THE THINKING RELATER

("The Specialist")

You're a private person who prefers a limited number of predictable, low-key, stable relationships and environments. You approach tasks and change cautiously: You like to do only what you know and know what you do.

Thinking Relaters are detail people who dislike ambiguity, changes, and surprises.

Your tendencies include these:

- liking checklists and by-the-numbers methods and schedules;
- preferring familiar relationships, situations, and tasks;
- disliking change, especially if it's unpredictable or unmanageable;
- minimizing risk before taking action;
- seeking approval for your consistency;
- being slow to act and react;

- having a defined scope of interests and activities; and
- taking an even narrower risk-minimizing approach when under pressure.

Your Growth Opportunities

With tasks: You can continue to improve by working on your pace. You're naturally slower to act than people with many of the other styles, so you need to strengthen your decision-making and problem-solving skills.

You're so detail-oriented that at times you fail to see the forest for the trees. Even worse, you may be so obsessed with details that you're looking at the leaves—or even at the veins in the leaves on these trees. Try to broaden your perspective. Do that by, first, focusing on the goal and then only on those details and actions that will help you attain it.

With people: You can benefit by expanding your horizons. You're most comfortable in dealing with what and whom you already know. But if you're to grow, you must learn to deal more effectively with people who are different. Try to reach out and look outward, too, rather than inward. Do this, and you'll have greater self-worth and confidence than those who are fear-driven and growth-resistant.

Personal Empowerment Pointers

- Interview and observe people who are quicker paced than you in making decisions and solving problems. Identify the three to five key actions that are essential to these skills—and then learn them.
- Guard against being overly focused on specifics. See if you can find a Socializing Director ("The Adventurer") who would coach you on how to be more global in your perspective.
- Be more genuinely open to people different from yourself. Identify at least one or two new growth goals each year that involve improving your adaptability.

THE THINKING THINKER

("The Analyst")

You're an individualist and a bit of a loner. Your desire for privacy colors your work and your relationships. In fact, you're so inward-focused that you may project a mystique in the eyes of your friends and associates.

You tend to be formal, quiet, and detached from people. You like to be in control of your work so you can minimize the chance of things going wrong. Cautious and intense, you value precision, accuracy, and impeccable personal habits. You evaluate others on how well and consistently they deliver on their promises. And you're quite careful about how many and what kind of commitments you yourself make.

Your tendencies include these:

- wanting to be right;
- having a reputation for acting and thinking logically;
- accumulating data, research, and information;
- seeking precision, discretion, and privacy;
- avoiding those who are irrational, volatile, or overly direct;
- being concerned about appearances;
- emphasizing reason and logic; and
- worrying excessively when under pressure and pulling back from risks or entanglements.

Your Growth Opportunities

With tasks: You're often indecisive, especially when dealing with complex, adverse, or risky situations. To avoid making mistakes or being embarrassed, you sometimes revert to your natural "worrywart" pattern. At such times, you may ponder all the options endlessly as you decide not to decide.

You can improve effectiveness by making decisions more quickly and knowing when you've collected enough information.

With people: Because you are deeply affected by criticism, you're less communicative than many. So you can benefit by learning to share your concerns and feelings and by expressing genuine appreciation for others. Also, you can lessen your inner tension and relax more if you can be less demanding and critical of yourself.

Personal Empowerment Pointers

- Manage your "worrywart" tendency. For example, when dealing with a new, possibly troubling, situation, write down the "worst thing that could possibly happen" and the "best thing." Identify the forces that can propel you toward the positive goal and those that must be dealt with to prevent the negative outcome. Then examine how each force can be capitalized upon, overcome, or neutralized. Ask a close friend for advice if the path is unclear.
- Be more communicative with others by sharing your thoughts and feelings more frequently and more deeply.
- Learn higher adaptability by observing others. The faster-paced, people-directing skills of the Director and the people-supporting ability of the Relater can be especially helpful.

THE DIRECTING THINKER

("The Mastermind")

Directing Thinkers are creators, not followers. You seek independence from constraints that might limit your performance. You like to be personally in control, but you're more into controlling procedures than controlling people. You can never get too much of quality, discovery, or originality.

You're very sensitive to conflict, resistance, and possible trouble, especially when they affect your goals.

Your tendencies include these:

- taking some calculated risks when making decisions;
- appearing focused and self-controlled with people;
- being very alert to conflict and resistance;
- preferring to work alone, or at the least with people of your choosing;
- being focused on the future, especially concerning ideas and opportunities;
- fearing losing your autonomy and individuality;
- enjoying planning, monitoring, and measuring; and
- becoming overly analytical—and possibly procrastinating—when under pressure.

Your Growth Opportunities

With tasks: Prone to overanalyze, you sometimes limit your own effectiveness. So you, too, can benefit by making quicker decisions and communicating more directly with your co-workers as you make those decisions.

With people: One of the most important changes you can make is to give yourself more credit and less grief. This would affirm yourself and counter your tendency to be overly self-critical. You'll also want to be more helpful and understanding of people who need hands-on coaching and counseling.

Personal Empowerment Pointers

- Work at being less guarded and more direct in your communication with others.
- Make sure you commit attitudinally to working closely with others on important tasks, not just menial ones.
- Monitor your tendency to be critical of yourself and others, especially under pressure.

THE SOCIALIZING THINKER

("The Assessor")

You're a highly analytical, quick-thinking person who can relate well to people if you want to. But you also prefer a private lifestyle shared with a limited number of close friends and co-workers.

As a people-oriented Thinker, your self-esteem is tied up in what you do and how well you do it. You're especially sensitive to how others view you and your work. So you seek to make an impact and get recognition for your contributions. When that isn't forthcoming, you suffer.

Your tendencies include these:

- being tense with yourself and others when under pressure;
- having a natural curiosity about people;
- being concerned about what people think, feel, and expect;
- having strong attachments to your personal interests;
- underestimating the time required to complete tasks;
- being intuitive and observant about situations and people;
- associating your self-worth with your work; and
- being intrigued by concepts, ideas, and processes.

Your Growth Opportunities

With tasks: You're an idea person who can profit by being more attentive to details and timely follow-through. Your curiosity sometimes leads to unpredictable digressions while you work. Thus, you can benefit by learning to pace yourself. Taking time-outs during the workday may help allay your natural intensity.

With people: Because you're intense by nature, you tend to be impatient with yourself and others, especially when things aren't going well. Therefore, focus on remaining positive when dealing with situations and people under pressure. If you can control your thoughts and emotions in such cases, you can then use your creativity to discover workable solutions.

Personal Empowerment Pointers

- Be attentive to what others expect. Deliver that first, before digressing into other areas that are likely to be of greater interest or curiosity to you.
- Stay focused on key priorities. Do that by sorting tasks into "immediate," "shorter-range," and "long-term" categories. Indicate those that you alone must do, those for which you share responsibility, and finally, those for which others have primary responsibility and your involvement is limited.
- Treat yourself to free time and recreation.

THE RELATING THINKER

("The Administrator")

You're the most inward-acting of all the behavioral styles. You like to work independently on familiar tasks that you can self-direct. That's how you avoid being embarrassed by inferior work or other surprises.

You're restrained, diplomatic, accommodating—and a true perfectionist with tasks and people. You always see a better way and a worse way, and you know which one you want to avoid.

Your tendencies include these:

- following established expectations and rules;
- preferring to have control over procedures;

- attending precisely to details and follow-through;
- disliking opposition, hostility, and adversity;
- desiring stability and clarity;
- being restrained, face-saving, and risk-averse;
- working comfortably in administrative or supporting roles; and
- becoming more reserved and indirect—perhaps even secretive and highly judgmental—when under pressure.

Your Growth Opportunities

With tasks: Because you're continually on the lookout for ideal solutions, you may miss the less-than-perfect opportunity. Or you may overlook the cumulative worth of piecemeal progress. You would benefit by developing more realistic expectations. For example, you should learn to manage risk and contingencies rather than avoiding them altogether, and get more comfortable with "trade-offs" when making decisions.

With people: Uncomfortable with in-depth involvement with people, you may need to work at building and using better social skills. You could benefit, for instance, by collaborating more and by being open and honest in expressing your thoughts. As those skills improve, so will your comfort with and enjoyment of differing types of people. That, in turn, can bolster your self-esteem.

Personal Empowerment Pointers

- Learn to adjust to less-than-perfect alternatives if they're available and workable.
- Be more open and forthright in expressing your thoughts.
- Be more genuinely open to people different from yourself. Identify at least one or two new growth goals each year that involve improving your adaptability.

6

◆

COPING PRODUCTIVELY
WITH THE OTHER STYLES

Gail sometimes told herself, only half-jokingly, that the greatest joy of being a corporate manager—after the car phone and use of the executive gym—was making the key personnel moves. She saw herself as a hands-on mentor, a hard-driving but helpful boss who'd given career boosts to many deserving employees. She was deadly serious about building the strongest department in the firm and one in which the bright and energetic would be rewarded.

Why, then, was this so *hard*?

She adored Bernice. They'd been friends and associates for years. Bernice was intelligent, knowledgeable, and absolutely passionate in her dedication to the firm. She was happy, humorous, and hopeful. And she shared Gail's fondness for ethnic food, epic movies, foreign travel, suspense novels, and long, looping walks through the park during which they talked about their ambitions.

Now Gail had a chance to make Bernice her second-in-command—but she was having trouble making a decision. The conflict tore at Gail, but she didn't know why. Out of frustration, she began questioning her own loyalty, her own motives. So she tried to reassess the situation objectively.

Certainly, she thought, Bernice had the skills, knowledge, and experience for the job. Besides, she was so well liked that her appointment would be applauded by the rank and file. Furthermore, the position was one Bernice had long wanted. And Gail, of course, loved her like a sister; they always had such a marvelous time together as friends.

But the more she thought about it, the more convinced Gail became that promoting Bernice would be a mistake. Gail, known as a stickler for results and for willingness to face the tough questions head-on, noted how Bernice would sometimes selectively listen for the "good" news, passing over other concerns. She remembered, for instance, Bernice's difficulty in doing performance evaluations on her subordinates, especially those who hadn't been doing so well.

True, Bernice was a marvelous motivator, always so upbeat—just her presence alone could energize a room full of people. And *articulate*! She could grasp a concept, talk it up, and inflate a group with enthusiasm better than anyone Gail knew. She could express a position so passionately that others, Gail included, would leave the room ablaze with motivation—until they later asked themselves, "What, exactly, did she *say*? Did she mention any studies, any facts, to back that up?"

It was always fun and exciting to have a friend who was bursting with a zillion ideas, even if few of them ever came to pass. In fact, Gail reflected on how she and Bernice might as well be on different planets as far as, for example, their approaches to decision-making.

Gail prided herself on being a quick study. She welcomed the chance to wrestle with problems, and whether they involved people or paper clips, it made little difference. Gail always cut to the heart of an issue and made a good, sound decision based on the known data. She didn't equivocate, and once she'd decided, she didn't look back either.

Bernice's problem-solving philosophy, on the other hand, was more along the lines of "Ready! Fire! Aim!" She would flit like a butterfly from problem to problem. She impulsively postponed many decisions while quickly making others, only to sometimes revisit those issues repeatedly when yet another idea occurred to her.

Her analysis done, Gail shook her head and sighed deeply. She saw only one clear, rational option for now: retain Bernice as a valued employee in her current role. Though she would try to keep her as a friend, Gail wouldn't promote Bernice to the number-two job.

All's not lost for Gail and Bernice as working partners. If they learn to adapt to one another's styles better, as we'll discuss in the next chapter, they can still form a sound, long-term relationship.

But for now, Gail's made the right call, and her dilemma shows how both bonds and barriers develop naturally among the four styles—and sometimes even between the same two people.

Such rapport, or tension, is not random. In fact, our compatibility is fairly predictable. **The Platinum**

Rule helps explain how we all behave according to certain principles. Once you understand and appreciate those principles, you will see that you and your co-workers aren't just a hodgepodge of individuals thrown together under one roof, but instead are more like the pieces of a puzzle that, with a little thought and practiced effort, can be made to fit together harmoniously.

The Platinum Rule gives you a more realistic idea of what to expect at work. Maybe you're struggling with a difficult boss. Or perhaps the co-worker at the desk next to yours is driving you crazy. Or you have a bright, but seemingly unmotivated, subordinate. In any case, you'll be able to figure out your colleagues at any level—and then act to lessen the tension.

So knowing and practicing **The Platinum Rule** will make you more effective—and make work more *fun*. If you're a manager, you'll see how to assign tasks and responsibilities more logically and manage people better. If you're a rank-and-filer, you'll see how you fit in and how you can improve your productivity. Regardless of your position, you'll be able to get along better and get better results.

Never has the ability to get along been more critical. As firms cut back, trim down, and reorganize, dealing well with the dwindling number of your fellow employees is increasingly important. As you learn what their pressure points are, you can take charge of your own compatibility and build bridges where there previously may have been deep chasms.

THE CHEMISTRY OF "LIKES" VERSUS "OPPOSITES"

Extroverts, such as Directors and Socializers, naturally gravitate toward other outgoing people in social situations. They send out instant signals by how loud and how fast they talk, how quick they are to give an opinion, sometimes even by the kind of clothes they wear.

The next time you're at a party, watch the people. You can almost see the Directors and Socializers being drawn together as if they were metal chips pulled by some giant magnet. They quickly size up one another and mentally decide, "There's somebody I can relate to. There's somebody like *me*!"

That's also true of the more reserved individuals, Relaters and Thinkers. An unspoken, unseen bond immediately connects them. They seem to be able to spot one another at ninety paces—maybe it's their body language, or their voices, or silent messages they send with their eyes. But, for sure, there's an undeniable comfort zone that attracts the like-minded.

So for both introverts and extroverts, there's this natural compatibility among their own kind—and, conversely, an innate tension between dissimilar types. Importantly, though, this usually differs—sometimes even radically—depending on whether the people are just together socially or working on a task. Rapport in *social* situations is no guarantee of rapport on *tasks*. In fact, often it's quite the reverse, as we'll see.

DEMYSTIFYING COMPATIBILITY

Compatibility, or the lack of it, is not such a mystery. Both rapport and tension are rather predictable, once you know what to look for. Here's the basic principle: In social situations (including interacting socially at work), like behavorial styles attract. People with similar habits and interests (for example, Gail and Bernice's fondness for walks, travel, ethnic food, and the same kinds of movies and novels) are drawn to one another as friends and acquaintances. We feel a comfort level, a high degree of satisfaction, in being with people who view the world along the same lines as we do, who respond to life in similar ways. There's a sense of satisfaction in knowing you're among people who prize what you prize, enjoy what you enjoy, play by roughly the same rules as you do.

If you're a Relater or a Thinker, you're a more structured person who's not fond of surprises. Thus, you find stable, predictable relationships more satisfying. You get your needs met by being around those who won't embarrass you by, say, showing up in a magenta sportscoat, or asking deeply personal questions upon first meeting you, or who tell loud, awful jokes or honk their car horns in tunnels.

Or maybe you're a faster-paced, more outgoing person, a Director or a Socializer who thinks life's too short to worry about whether your tires are properly inflated, your socks match your tie, or if free-range chicken grilled over mesquite twigs is better for your heart than the old-fashioned barnyard bird fried on the stove. Who in the heck's going to know or care 100 years from now, right? You're proud of your image of being someone who grabs for the gusto, and you naturally want to be among others who share the same habits and attitudes.

THE BIG TEN—AND HOW THEY PERFORM SOCIALLY

So what happens when these sometimes contradictory types get together? Well, the four basic behavioral styles mix and match into ten combinations. Behavioral-science research shows clearly which combinations—*prior* to use of **The Platinum Rule**—mesh or clash naturally.

For starters, people with *similar* tendencies are most compatible with one another socially. That's because those with common interests, habits, and approaches help reinforce each others' self-esteem.

So it won't surprise you to learn that the most naturally compatible combinations in social situations are:

Thinker-Thinker
Relater-Relater
Socializer-Socializer

Where, you ask, are the Directors? Well, they also tend to flock to one another—at least for a while. But remember, they possess such a strong competitiveness that even the Director-Director relationship isn't quite as naturally harmonious as the others.

That pairing does, however, show up under the next most naturally compatible category:

Director-Director
Relater-Thinker
Director-Socializer
Socializer-Relater

Compatibility doesn't come quite as naturally in these cases. But with effort, progress is possible and, in fact, success in working with less compatible individuals can be an esteem builder in each case.

Directors and Socializers share an outward focus and often similar interests. Relaters and Thinkers, on the other hand, are both inward-oriented and may like the same kinds of activities.

Both Socializers and Relaters aspire to be in a supportive relationship. Usually, though, it's the Relater who's in the giving role and the Socializer who's the receiver.

Meanwhile, the fast-paced, extroverted Directors and Socializers commonly find it hard to develop rapport with the easygoing, quieter Relaters and Thinkers, who are less decisive and enthusiastic. And the Relaters and Thinkers, in turn, find the Directors less desirable because they're too pushy, too loud, and often demand too much of them.

Therefore, of all ten combinations, these three pairs are often the least naturally compatible socially:

Director-Relater
Socializer-Thinker
Director-Thinker

To the Director, who just wants to get things done, and to the Socializer, who just wants to have fun, the cautious Thinker and steady Relaters can be drags. While Relaters often resign themselves to tolerate the forwardness of Directors and Socializers, the Thinker frequently just prefers to be alone.

What's more, even when relaxing, the Thinker wants to do all things right. Whether it's just grilling hot dogs, chatting about politics, or setting up the croquet wickets, the Thinker sets standards and judges himself and others by how they meet them. The Thinker is not living as much as he is, in the eyes of the Director or Socializer, just serving time. By and large, never the twain shall meet—at least unless and until **The Platinum Rule** is practiced.

On the positive side, though, there is a fascination factor in these three pairings, and bridges can be built. Most likely to succeed in doing so are those individuals who are positive and goal-oriented, who are always pushing themselves to become more effective. By contrast, if a person is fear-driven, he or she is probably going to be judgmental and defensive about the opposite styles. And that will likely be the death knell to a successful relationship with them.

Given positive energy, though, the natural differences can fuel attraction, particularly when one style sees what it can learn from another. A Director, for example, may see how he can become more patient and responsive to others by taking a cue from a Relater. A Relater, meanwhile, may be able to draw on the Director's strengths for taking charge and accepting risk.

Similarly, a sensitive Socializer can see how she can learn discretion from the Thinker, and the Thinker perceives that she can become more relaxed and sociable by being around the Socializer.

Perhaps the most difficult hurdles socially are posed by the Director-Thinker relationship. For it to work, both must yield their personal-control needs, with the Director deciding to give the type of space the Thinker needs, and the Thinker learning to be much more direct and open about his concerns with the Director.

But, to repeat, all ten combinations, from the most naturally harmonious to the most difficult, *can* be made to work. If people are willing to undergo a shift in attitude and work toward compatibility, as we'll examine in the next chapter, they can tap the power within themselves to be adaptable.

So that's how the combinations align in a social situation, whether at work or home or elsewhere. When it comes to performing tasks together, though, the picture often is very different.

IT'S DIFFERENT TASK-WISE

When it comes to tasks—whether it's doing a project at work, purchasing a family car, or just balancing the checkbook—the dynamics differ dramatically. Here, the "likes" who are drawn to one another socially don't necessarily attract as much as they compete or even conflict.

Now their similarities can get in the way because they have the same needs. After all, to complete a task, one must have resources, rewards, time, space, and attention. But there's only so much of those to go around.

So when those needs aren't met, tension and conflict can result. When one partner feels a need to "win," for instance, the other one may sense he or she's been shortchanged. The frequent outcome: resentment.

But, before getting into which pairs clash, let's look at the most naturally compatible combinations task-wise:

Thinker-Relater
Director-Relater
Socializer-Relater

See a pattern there? You bet! The good old Relater gets along with everybody in a task situation. He or she's the universal antidote for disharmony. It's the Relaters' most distinctive trait. They're supportive employees who exert a calming, stabilizing influence. Naturally interested in others and in making a contribution, they enjoy being productive partners. No wonder they're everybody's favorite.

The next most naturally compatible combinations, as far as working on tasks together, are:

Thinker-Thinker
Relater-Relater
Socializer-Thinker

Thinkers loom large in this second grouping. While not as easygoing as Relaters, they are sensitive to oth-

119

ers' feelings and have a passion for excellence that others usually recognize.

Interestingly, Thinkers figure in many of the least compatible combinations socially, but among the highest in tasks. That suggests that others appreciate the quality and thoroughness of their work, even if the Thinkers aren't always viewed as being a lot of laughs.

Last come those combinations that are often much less compatible because they tend to see one another as competitors:

Director-Director
Director-Thinker
Director-Socializer
Socializer-Socializer

Director-Director combinations work fairly well socially, as we've seen. But when it comes to tasks, a Director's competitive nature and need for control can stymie cooperation, especially with like-minded Directors.

As for the Director-Thinker, there's a fundamental clash in the Director's need for speed and control versus the Thinker's penchant for being slower-paced and systematic.

Notice that while the Socializer-Socializer pair was ranked as among the most socially compatible, now they are likely to be the least productive as far as working together on tasks. That's because neither is motivated to deal with task details.

Similarly, Directors and Socializers also have high social rapport but plummet to the lowest rungs of compatibility when tasks are involved. That's because, for one thing, they both tend to want to delegate. In addition, a "fight-or-flight" pattern can develop when performance difficulties occur.

That actually can occur among other combinations involving Directors and Socializers, too. The Director-Director scenario, in fact, may evolve into something approaching a state of war. But when the Socializer is involved, on the other hand, he or she is likely to go off in another direction, seeking solace for his or her bruised ego from other types who will provide the approval the Socializer needs.

In truth, a "fight-or-flight" response to stress can occur for all types, including Relaters and Thinkers, when they bump up against the Directors or Socializers, or even against each other. But it's less obvious with Relaters and Thinkers because both are more inward-acting. Being less direct, they don't readily show their feelings.

For example, Relaters typically back off and tolerate such stress by seeking a safe haven in their own work, though they may be tense and uncomfortable just below the surface. The Thinker, by contrast, tends to fight back—but indirectly, almost invisibly. He or she generally chooses not to get angry, as a Director might, but instead may quietly plot ways to "get even." This quiet form of revenge might involve withholding information or needed know-how, or they might make themselves unavailable when their help is needed.

So, strange as it seemed to her at the time, it wasn't really odd that Gail enjoyed being friends with Bernice but was uncomfortable about turning over certain tasks to her. Gail, a likely Director, knew at some level that Bernice, a probable Socializer, and she weren't as naturally well suited for accomplishing certain tasks as they were for enjoying one another's company.

But don't give up yet on Bernice—or on lots of others whose personal style may not be a perfect fit with the situation. In the next chapter we'll look in detail at ways to adapt to the other styles so that these natural barriers can be surmounted. In truth, with some effort at understanding and applying **The Platinum Rule**, you can change your compatibility so you can work successfully with anyone.

ONE COMMON TASK: NEGOTIATING

One task that brings these personality distinctions into sharper focus is negotiating. By definition, it always involves at least one other person and usually entails a conflict, or a potential conflict.

And despite what you might think, we're all negotiators. Just about every job involves some negotiating. Often it isn't called that. It isn't usually done sitting on opposite sides of a big oak table, with maybe a lawyer or two by your side.

But it's negotiating just the same when you make your case for more overtime pay, or you ask the company's food manager to try to improve the cafeteria selection, or try to get a bigger budget for your department. In truth, we all negotiate informally almost every day on something or other, and our knowledge of personal styles can have a huge impact on our success.

A true story:

Gary is a hard-driving insurance executive with an intimidating, take-no-prisoners approach to competitors. He gets things done quickly, sometimes brusquely. That style had always gotten him good bottom-line results. Or at least it did until he encountered a conservative, buttoned-down president of another firm, which owed Gary's business $2 million.

Gary desperately needed the money paid in a lump sum, not installments. Three times Gary met with the other person. Three times Gary came on strong, and three times his counterpart, who didn't like to be bullied, dug in his heels.

Gary faced failure. Maybe even financial disaster. Then he learned about **The Platinum Rule**—and soon he had his $2 million in hand.

How? At their fourth meeting, Gary modified his approach, not his message. He made the other person feel more at ease. He slowed the pace. He provided more information, went into more detail about why a lump-sum payment made sense for both of them.

Tension went down. Cooperation went up. And Gary went home with the $2 million instead of delay and possible litigation.

Gary, of course, was right in seeing that the other individual needed special handling. But here's the point: *We all do.*

Gary now realized that he was a Director and that his counterpart was probably a Thinker who wasn't trying to block payment of the money but simply didn't understand and therefore did not appreciate Gary's approach to the problem.

That's the kind of potential that exists when you can get a good sense of how to motivate each of the four basic behavioral styles. Notice that Gary didn't abandon his principles, or lie, or do anything manipulative. Instead, he simply observed his adversary and then acted to make that person more comfortable.

Many of us go about negotiating wrongheadedly, as Gary did initially. We often assume that everybody has the same goal: grabbing as much as they can while leaving us next to nothing.

That's how we usually think of it. But that attitude is almost sure to breed tension and leave at least one side—and sometimes both—disappointed. Instead, we suggest using **The Platinum Rule** to make your negotiating smoother and the outcome more mutually beneficial.

NEGOTIATING EFFECTIVELY WITH THE FOUR STYLES

For starters, think for a moment about how each of the four basic styles is likely to negotiate. What most motivates them?

You already know how important winning is to the Director. They're fighters; they expect to conquer or be conquered in the negotiating room. To them, win-win may equate with wishy-washy. Winning to Directors means that someone else is likely to lose.

But *think*. Could that be the Director's vulnerability? Is there a way to use that mind-set to your advantage? We'll come back to that in a moment.

Or consider the Socializer. It won't surprise you that as negotiators, as in most everything else, Socializers are positive and enthusiastic, so positive and enthusiastic about their latest proposal that they may not be paying attention to the nuts and bolts. Keep that in mind.

The Relaters' idea of winning is, of course, to have everybody be happy, even if the Relaters themselves don't gain personally. So they're just the opposite of the Directors in that—and most every other—regard.

And the Thinkers can be—surprise! surprise!—a bit rigid as negotiators. They're more into principle than pragmatism; they negotiate on fact, not relationships. Knowing that, you'll have an advantage, as we'll see.

So each style has a different goal and approach when negotiating. The Director wants victory, with a capital "V"; the world, in his eyes, consists of winners and losers—and he knows which he wants to be. The Socializer seeks to be embraced by others, to win glory. The Relater, meanwhile, wants peace and amiability. And the Thinker covets order and yearns for established procedures and a factual, logical outcome. As Roger Dawson, author of *Secrets of Power Negotiating for Salespeople*, points out, "Win-win negotiating can only come when you understand that people don't want the same things in negotiation."

So negotiating well is not just a matter of dickering over the terms of the agreement. And it's not just about getting what you want. Successful negotiating comes from also being concerned about what the other person wants. It's **The Platinum Rule** applied to the ancient art of bargaining.

The skillful negotiator uses his or her knowledge of **The Platinum Rule** personal styles to forge a win-win agreement. He or she doesn't just ask, What can I get from them? Instead, the astute negotiator asks this key question: What can I give them that won't take away from my position?

Let's say you're a landlord trying to lease an office suite. The rent, length of the lease, level of amenities, and occupancy date are all up in the air.

First, you're dealing with a Director. You know she's got to come away looking like the winner. So she may not be satisfied unless she can beat you down on your price, right? Right.

Because you understand personal styles, though, you know that a shortcoming in the Director's approach is that she can obsess on one or two issues at the expense of others. You also know that to feel that she's won, this Director is probably going to want to see that you've had to concede on some points.

So what's the answer? For starters, don't talk "win-win"; you'll sound like a wimp. Instead, ask for the full amount of rent, then tell her how much it hurts to back down and give her the price she demands. But, meanwhile, go for a shorter lease, less opulent amenities, and perhaps an earlier-than-scheduled occupancy date so you can recoup some, or all, of what you conceded rent-wise.

The Director will feel she beat you, and she can boast for years that she set her price limit, stuck to it, and triumphed by using her shrewdness and forcefulness. But the real bottom line is that you adapted.

You allowed her to get what was important to her while meeting your own needs, too.

Similarly, if your potential lessee was a Socializer, you'd know he primarily wants to inspire people, and dearly loves to turn them on to a particular idea. Maybe his notion is that this office suite can become the showplace of his firm's network of offices nationwide, and that he'd love to bask in the glory of its grandeur.

Your knowledge of behavioral styles tells you that once the Socializer locks onto a concept, everything else—including money and logic—tends to take a backseat. So give him what he wants. Encourage him to dream of a corporate Taj Mahal. Agree to put solid-gold faucets and Italian marble in the washrooms. Explore the possibility of a new foyer that would make King Tut proud. But while you agree to meet *his* goals by giving him a suite to die for, get *your* price.

A Relater, in his heart of hearts, wants all the world to be a warm and fuzzy place. He may want this office suite, but even more he wants these negotiations and what follows to be noncontentious. So what do you do? Go slow, go easy, be as tenant-friendly as you can possibly be. Cater to his goals—and you'll likely achieve your own as a payoff.

The Thinker, to the contrary, doesn't care as much about warm fuzzies, doesn't want a deep or lasting relationship. She wants facts, procedures, and a sense of progress. So, again, do your best to meet her needs. Pie charts, printouts, graphs, testimonials, whatever it takes to give the Thinker a sense that you've done an enviably thorough job of research, that this suite's the most value for the money, that it's the only logical choice of a reasonable person. Do that, and the other points—the ones important to you—won't matter so much to her.

In short, then, being successful at negotiations is, first, a matter of perception. Then, adaptation. Each of the four basic styles perceives success differently. So if you're a different style from the person across the table, you're probably not seeking the same thing.

Using **The Platinum Rule**, though, you can figure out how he defines success. Then you can adapt and help your adversary reach his goal, not by forcing him off his bargaining position, but by concentrating on his interests while, of course, seeing that your own are taken care of, too.

7

◆

HOW TO ADAPT TO ANYONE . . .
AND RETAIN YOUR OWN IDENTITY

An important client is on the phone. "Hey! We've been talking about getting together," he reminds you. "Here's an idea: Let's grab an early breakfast Saturday and then hit the first tee by seven A.M. We'll beat the crowds that way and get in a full eighteen holes before noon. Heck, maybe we can even get in another round after that."

You're not a morning person, to put it mildly. Or, for that matter, much of a golfer. So the idea of getting up at, say, 5:30 on a Saturday to have breakfast at six followed by as much as thirty-six holes of golf is a prospect only slightly more pleasant than a root canal.

But if it was *important*, if a possible big sale hung in the balance, if your career could be affected, you'd show up, wouldn't you? You'd be willing to adapt to meet your client's wishes.

Or what if your boss comes over to your desk? He's holding your long-awaited report, and he says, "It

looks to me like you made a bad mistake in these figures about the project's cost!"

You spent *days* on that report. You checked and
double-checked those figures—they *can't* be wrong!
You're *sure* of it.

But what do you do? Do you leap to your feet and
angrily challenge your boss's statement? Do you
stride out of the room in a huff? Or do you calmly listen to him and try to understand his perspective,
opening yourself to his feedback?

You'd make an effort to be open if it was important
enough to keep good relations with the boss, wouldn't
you? Of course.

WHAT IS ADAPTABILITY?

That's adaptability. To be willing and able to bend a
bit if that's what it takes to make a better relationship. It's a way to work better with a specific person
or in a certain situation. It means thinking before you
act. It means not just doing or saying the first thing
that comes to your mind.

The truth is: You do it all the time.

You may show a different side of yourself when
you go to the boss's house for dinner than when you
go to a friend's place for a game of cards. Or you may
act differently at a ball game than you do at a business meeting. And do you behave the same at an art
museum as you do at a Halloween party? Of course
not.

You adapt because you sense that a different type

of behavior is called for if you're to be successful and to be accepted. And you're right. The key point is: You can sharpen that skill of knowing when and how to adapt. You can learn to adapt to all kinds of people and situations. As a result, you can find success and acceptance you never dreamed of.

THE MEANING OF ADAPTABILITY

Every savvy businessperson knows that if you're trying to conduct a deal in, say, Japan, you must learn to understand and respect certain cultural differences. Perhaps you learn to bow. Or eat with chopsticks. Or negotiate in the more low-key, accommodating style. Why? Because it's respectful and it's *important.*

It's also respectful and important to learn to adapt to the personal styles in your own workplace. More than you may realize, your happiness, your effectiveness, and your future will be affected by how well you get along with people. And how well you get along depends in large measure on your ability to adapt.

An example:

> Deborah is a businesswoman who exudes warmth, even over the phone. She likes restaurant meetings and usually arrives early. When you meet her for the first time, she shakes your hand enthusiastically, asks if you like rum, then orders a drink she is certain you'll enjoy as she proceeds to relate

the story of her first experience with that drink in New Orleans.

Your lunch lasts $2\frac{1}{2}$ hours: 15 minutes on business, 20 minutes on new jokes, and the rest on Deborah's accomplishments and interests. During the lunch, she makes friends with the manager and three waitresses, including one who bumped into her as she was gesturing wildly during one of her punchlines.

Clearly, Deborah is a hard-core Socializer. Unless you, too, are a Socializer (in which case, the meeting may last 4 hours instead of $2\frac{1}{2}$), you'll need to adapt if this meeting is to have a successful business outcome.

If you're not a very adaptable person, if you respond uniformly to all personalities, you're not going to have much luck with Deborah. Or, for that matter, with about three-fourths of the population. You're going to be undermining your own efforts to build rapport.

The truly adaptable person, though, meets the other person's needs *and* his or her own. Our research indicates that:

- most people aren't as adaptable as they think,
- but they can learn to better develop their adaptability.

This chapter will show how and when to adapt your style to connect with anyone in the workplace. Many of us do this instinctively to a slight degree when we talk a bit more with chatty people or are more quiet when with deep thinkers. But you're going to learn how to operate more systematically within the other person's comfort zone.

Even as you alter your own style to mesh better with others, it's important to maintain your own identity. Someone who is *too* adaptable can be seen as not being genuine, as insincere. So this chapter will help you modify your "spots," not change them.

ATTITUDE AND APTITUDE

Adaptability doesn't mean mimicking another person's style. It doesn't mean abandoning your identity or your good business sense. It just means adjusting your openness and directness, your pace and priority, to make this relationship work.

There are two parts to being adaptable: being *willing* and being *able*.

Willingness, or "flexibility," means you are open to the possibility of adapting. You've got a positive *attitude* about adjusting your behavior in a given situation. This is a sign of maturity.

Studies show that highly flexible people tend to be:

Confident:	Resourceful, have trust in their judgments.
Tolerant:	Don't judge differing opinions, practices.
Empathic:	Relate to what others are feeling.
Positive:	Hopeful about people, situations, and life.

Respectful: Understand, accept, and appreciate others.

If you want to be more flexible, those are the traits you should cultivate. Conversely, inflexible people often are rigid, overly competitive, discontent, and unapproachable. They also tend to see the world only in terms of blacks and whites instead of gray; that is, what's been referred to as "the tyranny of either-or thinking" (versus the magnificence of a "both-and" mind-set or approach).

On the other hand, "versatility" is the aptitude for adapting. This is not an attitude, but a set of skills, and thus it takes time to acquire. The characteristics that encompass such skills include:

Resilience: Emotional strength to rebound from setbacks and overcome barriers.

Vision: Ability to foresee opportunities, create alternatives.

Attentiveness: Awareness of people's feelings and a good sense of timing about your own actions.

Competence: Effectively making decisions, solving problems, and handling situations.

Self-correction: Ability to evaluate your behavior clearly and to learn from your mistakes.

These are traits to sharpen to become more versatile. Some qualities, on the other hand, seem to prevent people from being effective adapters. Those include bluntness, resistance to change, single-mindedness, un-reasonable risk-taking, and subjectivity, which is the inability to see the world from any perspective but your own. If they describe you, you may want to try to reduce or eliminate those traits, or at least seek to keep them from getting in the way of your versatility.

ACHIEVING A BALANCE

Relationships, like money, must be managed. The highly adaptable person meets the other person's needs and his own. Through attention and practice, you can learn to do that. You can see when no change is called for and when a modest compromise is appropriate. Or even when the situation calls for a fairly radical adjustment to another person's behavioral style.

Learn these skills, and you'll learn to handle relationships in a way that allows everyone to win. Learn these skills, and you'll learn to make everyone more comfortable. Learn these skills, and you'll truly be practicing **The Platinum Rule**.

But adaptability is more than just a game plan for being named "Most Congenial." Because, most of all, it's *practical* and *powerful*. It helps you handle tense situations and to deal better with difficult people. But it also affects how others view their relationship with you. Raise your adaptability, and trust and credibility skyrocket. Lower your adaptability, and they go down dramatically.

MANAGING YOUR COMPATIBILITY

Adaptability, in essence, means managing your own compatibility. No one style is naturally more adaptable than another, and the adjustments will vary for each of us.

That's because adaptability is something you *choose*. You can opt to be quite adaptable with one person today and less adaptable with that same individual tomorrow. You can choose to be adaptable in one situation and unadaptable in another.

A Socializer, for example, can adapt to a Thinker by talking less, listening more, and focusing on the task at hand. Or a Relater can adapt to a Director by giving information succinctly, trying not to be overly casual or sociable, and quickening the pace. And Directors can adapt to Socializers by taking the time to listen to their dreams and getting to know them.

GETTING STARTED ON ADAPTING

In Chapter 4, you learned how to read people quickly. You saw how to study their speech and other clues, then pinpoint their style by figuring out the degree to which they're direct or indirect, open or guarded.

Similarly, you can learn to adapt based on just a few clues. Then you can fine-tune your adaptation later as other pieces of the personality puzzle fall into place.

For starters, whatever your style, you can take

some simple actions that will help you improve your adaptability.

A CHECKLIST FOR EXPANDING ADAPTABILITY

Relaters Can . . .	*Socializers Can* . . .
Say no occasionally	Control time and emotions
Take some risks	Try to be more objective
Delegate to others	Follow up on promises, tasks
Accept logical changes	Concentrate on the job at hand
Verbalize their feelings to appropriate people	Try a more logical approach
Finish tasks without oversensitivity to others' feelings	Spend more time checking, specifying, organizing

Thinkers Can . . .	*Directors Can . . .*
Openly show concern and appreciation of others	Project a more relaxed image by pacing themselves
Initiate new projects	Become more open, patient listeners
Use policies as guidelines, not laws	Develop patience, sensitivity, and empathy
Collaborate by seeking common ground	Genuinely compliment others
Occasionally try shortcuts and time-savers	Act less hastily, more cautiously
Make timely decisions	Identify with the group

ADAPTING IN SPECIFIC SITUATIONS

Okay, so those are some things you can do unilaterally to make your style more compatible with the world at large. But how do you adapt in specific situations?

Let's say it's Deirdre's first day on the job as co-manager of Marketing. She'll be working with Henry, who's been the sole manager until now.

Deirdre's a Relater. She and Henry have only met a couple of times previously, so she doesn't really know him or his style very well. She walks into Henry's office through an open door, smiles, and extends her hand. "Nice to see you again. I'm looking forward to working with you!" she says brightly.

Henry stands up and shakes her hand but says gruffly, "Didn't my secretary tell you I've got a meeting in a few minutes? If you'll wait outside, I'll see you in an hour or so. Didn't my secretary tell you that people schedule appointments with me? I'm busy most of this week. Maybe we can talk sometime next week."

Deirdre, being a student of **The Platinum Rule**, can see right away that Henry is no Relater. He's fast-paced and task-oriented rather than people-oriented.

There are probably two main ways she might respond:

Her natural response, which we'll call *Deirdre No. 1*, might be: "Gee, Henry, I'm sorry to have interrupted. Forgive me! Sure, I'll talk with your secretary and see if we can set something up in a week or two when your schedule is more clear."

Or perhaps she could respond another way, which we'll call *Deirdre No. 2*: "Well, I don't want to interrupt your work. But we do have some business we've got to get to soon. Others are depending on us. Have you given any thought to a plan for how we can work on the transition to a comanagership? If you have anything for me to read or do on it, I'll begin right now."

Which scenario shows the most adaptability? You might see Deirdre No. 1 as being most adaptable: She actually agreed to do what Henry wanted, whether it was reasonable or not. But that's not really what's meant by adaptability. If she'd done that, she would have been acquiescent, as a Relater naturally tends to be.

Instead, Deirdre No. 2, sensing that her normal style wouldn't suffice, modified her behavior to communicate better with fast-paced, task-oriented Henry. She spoke up with a strong, yet positive, response. She became somewhat more fast-paced and task-oriented herself.

NOT WIMPING OUT

Deirdre No. 2 confidently expressed her own interests that affected both of them and their business at hand. For sure, she would gain Henry's attention and cooperation much faster that way.

So adapting doesn't mean wimping out, giving in, rolling over. It does mean, for starters, recognizing whether the other person is fast-paced or slow-paced, task-oriented or people-oriented, and then moving in that direction.

Deirdre had only a few moments to scope out Henry's characteristics and adapt to them. So she naturally—and wisely—made a quick, accurate diagnosis about his pace and priorities.

But let's say she and Henry do start working together often and she gets more of a chance to observe his personal style. If she's to succeed in her new job, adapting to Henry is going to be an ongoing, important challenge. So she wants to take adaptability a step further.

As she goes into the first few meetings with him, she looks for other signs. She notices that Henry sits behind his desk rather than on the couch or at the small table in his office where they might be closer. Usually, after a glance at his watch, he begins the meeting.

Henry: "Frankly, Deirdre, you're not ready for this job. I've seen nice young people like you promoted over their heads before. It won't work. It always ends badly. You ought to go talk to the bonehead who gave you this promotion and see if there aren't other alternatives for you. In short, I don't need you here. You won't like it, and in the long run you'll hurt yourself by being here because there's nothing for you to do, and even if there were, you and I would be like oil and water. That's blunt, I know. But I believe in speaking plainly, and so I'm telling you this for your own good."

Deirdre listens, trying to keep her anger under control and trying to figure out her best response quickly. Henry is *very* direct: assertive, aggressive, confrontational. He's not at all shy about exercising control.

He's also guarded rather than open: He's task-oriented, disciplined about time, somewhat formal and proper. Though he's told her that she'll never fit in, he said almost nothing about his style or how he sees the job. In fact, he hasn't shared any personal feelings about his work, the company, or her.

Henry, Deirdre realizes, is direct and guarded: a Director. Deirdre mulls over her options quickly. Her instinctual response as a Relater would be:

Deirdre No. 1: "Hmmm. That's interesting. Perhaps you're right. I do want the job but, on the other hand, we've certainly got to get along if this coman-

141

ager arrangement is going to work. And I appreciate your words about my long-term future here. Let me think about what you've said, and I'll get back to you."

But she knows that won't do. Henry would just steamroller over her like he's probably done to so many others. Instead, she needs to get more on his wavelength by becoming more direct and less open.

So she might say:

Deirdre No. 2: "Let me remind you, Henry, that it was headquarters that assigned me to this job. Obviously, somebody upstairs believes I have something to offer and that you do need help managing the department. Frankly, if they thought you were doing such a terrific job already, they wouldn't have sent me. Therefore, I expect your cooperation. I want this to work and am doing my best to make it so. However, if you don't play ball, I'll have no choice but to tell the vice president you're being resistant. And *that* won't be good for you or your career, Henry. Not good at all."

That would be very direct, but overly controlling. That would be talking to him like a Director, all right. And it might mean the end of any opportunity for genuine cooperation between Henry and Deirdre. "Out-Henrying" Henry would probably be the death knell to any hopes of effectively comanaging the department.

So, wisely, Deirdre opts for a third approach, like this:

Deirdre No. 3: "I understand your concern, Henry, because I know how committed you are to the success of our department. If I were you, I also might be worried about whether I was turning my 'baby' over to someone who maybe wasn't quite ready to assume such responsibility. But, let's face it, Henry, I wouldn't be here unless other people, several levels above us, thought I was ready. So I have an obligation to justify their confidence in me. I want to do that by learning as much as I can from you. You've got the experience, and I want to work with you. I want to help sustain the progress that you've made in the years you've been here.

"And you're right—sure, we're different. But think of the synergy the two of us can create. We can make Marketing a standout that'll be the envy of every other department in this firm."

What did Deirdre do in this last response?

She modified her openness and directness to be more in line with Henry's. She decreased her openness by being more businesslike, having more of a logical, factual orientation. She increased her directness by speaking at a faster pace, giving a recommendation rather than asking for an opinion, facing conflict head-on, using direct statements rather than posing questions, and challenging him tactfully.

Deirdre also showed empathy for Henry that was missing in the earlier responses. If you were Henry, wouldn't you be more inclined to work with Deirdre No. 3?

Sure. Both gained by Deirdre's ability and willingness to modify her style. Henry could at least see the potential in working with this savvy woman who wouldn't be pushed around and who understood and appreciated him.

Deirdre now knew that, though it would take some work, she could coexist with Henry. After all, she was able to get him to back off his initial take-no-prisoners approach. She learned that he respects force, and so she was a bit forceful with him. But she also showed him that she appreciates him. The Henry-Deirdre relationship was transformed from a potentially bitter clash into what's potentially a lasting win-win situation.

Deirdre adapted well to Henry, who is a Director. The general strategies for adapting to a Director are:

To Adapt to Directors

Be efficient and competent by:

- supporting their goals and objectives when possible;
- keeping your relationship businesslike;
- using facts—not personal feelings—if you disagree;
- being precise, efficient, and well organized;
- recommending alternate actions with brief supporting analysis;
- getting to the point quickly; and
- stressing competitive results and growth opportunities.

But just think, if Henry had also practiced **The Platinum Rule**, he would have figured out that Deirdre was a Relater. Can you imagine how much less friction there would have been, how much more quickly they could have come to terms, if Henry also had been willing to adapt?

TO ADAPT TO RELATERS

Be warm and sincere by:

- supporting their feelings by showing personal interest when possible;
- assuming they'll take things personally;
- allowing them time to trust you;
- discussing personal feelings—not facts—when you disagree;
- moving along in a slower, informal, but steady manner;
- showing that you're "actively" listening; and
- giving assurances that risk will be minimized or handled as reasonably as possible.

PLANNING THE PICNIC

Another example:

Thom is an up-and-coming young manager at a growing electronics firm. He's also a Thinker, so he prides himself on attention to detail, thoroughness, and following procedures. And he's committed to a career at this company, which really puts a high priority on employee morale.

Thom isn't thrilled when his department head asks him to spearhead plans for a company-wide picnic. Previously, each department had its own picnic. But now the firm's president, trying to encourage cohesiveness, wants everybody to picnic together.

Thom has great organizing skills, says Thom's boss,

who adds, "Besides, you won't be doing it alone. Joel, over in Sales, is going to be your cochair. You'll probably need to touch base with him very soon."

Thom goes looking for Joel in his office. Thom sees that Joel's desk is cluttered and disorganized. Numerous plaques and certificates cover the walls. A small straw sombrero, a souvenir of some Mexican junket, sits cockeyed atop a bowling trophy. Behind it there's a picture of Joel performing at what appears to be a karaoke bar. If this office could speak, Thom thinks, it would say, "Notice me." Thom, who's naturally much more understated and reserved, feels his stomach tighten.

Joel is talking animatedly on the phone but he waves Thom on in. When the phone call ends, Joel gives Thom a warm handshake, makes lots of eye contact, and gently slaps Thom on the shoulder as he invites him to take a seat.

Though Thom hasn't met him before, he soon knows more than he needs or wants to know about Joel's family and his financial and professional history. Joel's fast-paced delivery is lively, stimulating, and upbeat as he laughs, gestures, and seemingly exaggerates a lot. Thom suspects that Joel is very good at sales, though Thom's already fighting an urge to think that anybody that friendly is a phony, or what Thom thinks of as being "all hat, no cowboy."

Finally, when Thom starts to tell him about the picnic and how the two of them need to get started, Joel suddenly cools off. He acts very unimpressed and nonchalant.

"Geez, Thom, that's still six weeks away. Besides, it's no big deal, right? I mean, we get some burgers and buns—and balloons for the kids. And"—he snaps his fingers—"we got it handled. It's no biggie."

Now Thom's really concerned. Here's the guy he's counting on to help put this thing together, and he's acting supremely relaxed, almost as if he can't be bothered.

But Thom knows it's little things like picnics that affect how you're viewed by the managers, and that a screw-up here when the big boss is watching could have longer-range consequences for both of them.

Joel just doesn't realize the importance of the assignment. With only six weeks remaining, Thom thinks, we've got to nail down a site, get the food ordered, arrange entertainment and a host of other things. In fact, we should have a schedule already drawn up, with deadlines and responsibilities attached.

As a Thinker, Thom's natural response to the Joel conflict would most likely be to withdraw. He'd be tempted just to write Joel off as a lightweight and say to himself, "If he's such a hopeless bumbler that he won't jump in and help me get this thing handled, then I'll just have to do it all myself. In fact, I'll probably be better off."

Remembering The Platinum Rule

But then Thom remembers **The Platinum Rule**. He knows that Joel is open (he's already told Thom his life story) and direct (he was quick to sound off on just about everything, including how picnics ought to be spontaneous, not planned). Open and direct? Right. So he's a Socializer, the type that Thom often has the most trouble with.

Thom doesn't want to blow this by getting uptight

and walking away without a promise of cooperation. So he decides to adjust his response. Thom will speed up his pace, act a little looser, show an interest in Joel as well as in getting the job done, and show that he's concerned with people as well as tasks.

"Maybe you're right, Joel. This assignment isn't going to become the highlight of your résumé or mine. But you gotta do what you gotta do, I guess."

Joel nods.

"But I can tell that you're a people person. And our mission, if we choose to accept it," he continues, with a chuckle, "is to put on a picnic where everyone'll have a good time, morale'll be improved, and so on. Plus, did you know that the company president is the one who came up with this idea? It's probably not the job you or I would've picked for ourselves, but I suspect the Big Guy's going to be watching.

"How 'bout this for an idea: Let me make a few calls about the availability of a site and get an estimate of how much and what kind of food we're going to need. Maybe you could do some noodling about games and activities. Then we'll compare notes in—what?—a week or so?"

What did Thom do? He avoided confrontation. He tried to be more sociable. He sent out signals that he appreciates Joel as a person and that, even though they have differing priorities, they could work together and maybe help themselves in the eyes of top management.

Thom still isn't sure how much of a help Joel is going to be, especially on follow-through. But at least Thom hasn't burned any bridges. He's kept open the possibility that the picnic project can be turned into a mutual win instead of a hopeless clash of styles.

And at their next meeting, Thom may be able to take their relationship a step further.

TEMPORARY CHANGES IN APPROACH

Thom correctly saw what he had to do to avoid alienating Joel. He didn't abandon his principles. He didn't change his personality. But because there was so much at stake, he did make some temporary changes in his approach. He used some classic strategies to adapt to an obvious Socializer.

Generally, here's what you would do:

To Adapt to Socializers

Show interest in them by:

- supporting their opinions, ideas, and dreams when possible;
- being upbeat, stimulating, and fast-paced;
- tolerating digressions and not hurrying a discussion;
- trying not to argue—you'll seldom win;
- being enthusiastic, spontaneous, and casual;
- explaining how action can enhance their image and visibility; and
- sparing them the details.

If Joel had also been adhering to **The Platinum Rule**, he could have helped by moving a bit toward

Thom's position. He could have seen that Thom was indirect and guarded—a Thinker. Then he could have altered his own style. He could have talked less, listened more, and focused on the facts. That would have practically ensured that the picnic would be a well-planned, well-run, fun-filled affair and a feather in both their caps.

Joel could have used some of the following strategies to put Thom at ease:

To Adapt to Thinkers

Show yourself to be thorough and well prepared by:

- supporting their organized, thoughtful approach when possible;
- showing commitment through your actions, not just words;
- being detailed, accurate, and logical;
- listing advantages and disadvantages of any plan;
- providing solid, tangible evidence;
- adhering to established procedures; and
- giving assurances that decisions won't backfire on them.

There's hope for Thom and Joel and the picnic. Actually, differences in style can bring a zest to problem-solving. The whole *can* be more than the sum of its parts. Often stylistic differences, if they can be bridged, will lend an energy to a team effort that similar styles would not. (See Chapter 8.)

So you see, flexibility doesn't mean "imitation" of the other person's style. It doesn't mean being wishy-washy or two-faced or trying to be something you're not.

Deirdre, for example, didn't try to coerce Henry. She wouldn't have felt comfortable doing so—and it probably wouldn't have worked. Instead, she adjusted her style in a way that put her more on Henry's wavelength.

Similarly, Thom, though he might have been tempted, didn't spin on his heel and walk out. Nor did he cave in and agree that the picnic planning should be left to whim. He made an effort to meet Joel at least halfway. That's what adaptability—and **The Platinum Rule**—are all about.

ANTIDOTE TO CONFLICT

The antidote to most personality conflicts is just that obvious. Cultivate a style that's adaptable. Give your full attention to the other person and seek to cooperate, not confront.

Adaptability is the key to success with people. Some of us do it naturally; others must work at it because life-long habits of competition, conflict avoidance, or resistance to change are not altered overnight. But you *can* do it *if* you're committed, *if* you use both your head and your heart.

Which reminds us of a parable conveying ancient wisdom about adaptability. Two Buddhist monks were walking through the woods one day when they came to a mountain stream rushing over large boulders.

A poor peasant woman was standing at the edge, wanting to cross but afraid of the current. The monks had taken a vow of celibacy, which included a pledge of not physically touching a woman.

Nonetheless, one of the monks picked up the woman and carried her across the stream. The woman thanked him when they reached the other side, and the two holy men continued on their way. Neither said a word about the incident.

Finally, after a couple of hours, the second monk asked, "How could you pick up that woman and carry her across the stream? Don't you remember your vow never to touch a woman?"

The other monk replied, "I put her down several hours ago. Why haven't you?" The first monk knew he hadn't broken the *spirit* of the monastery's rules; clearly, he'd just made a wise, practical, people-oriented choice. He had decided to be flexible by helping another human being in need but without abandoning his beliefs or trying to be something he wasn't.

Likewise, adaptability means changing your behavior when it makes sense to do so. It means being open to alternatives. It means breaking from past practices when conditions change and when, as a result, different "rules" are called for. Above all, adaptability means having a flexible, positive, humane attitude in order to bring about good results.

8

♦

USING INDIVIDUAL DIFFERENCES TO BRING OUT THE BEST IN GROUPS

Imagine the setting: A corporate meeting room.

Imagine the task: To organize a big, new project.

Imagine the committee members: A Director, a Socializer, a Relater, and a Thinker.

Imagine what happens next: Contention? Chaos? Homicide?

You can probably envision the Director closing the door and announcing, "All right, everybody, let's get this show on the road! Here's my plan."

At which point the Socializer might pipe up, "Hey, who died and made you King of the World? We've got plenty of time to work this thing out. Speaking of time, that reminds me of a story about this guy with one of those Mickey Mouse watches who went into . . ."

This chapter includes material from *The Dynamic Decision Maker: Five Decision Styles for Executive and Business Success*, by M. J. Driver, K. R. Brousseau, and P. L. Hunsaker. San Francisco: Jossey-Bass, 1993.

The Thinker, who's been listening patiently, interjects, "It seems to me the first thing this committee has got to agree on is a structure and a mission. So, first, let's decide . . ."

The Socializer continues telling his story while the Thinker is pleading for order and the Director is getting red in the face at what he sees as these needless digressions. The Relater, meanwhile, implores, "Please, let's try to get along and work as a team. I'm sure we all have contributions to make."

The truth is that natural allies and antagonists abound among the four basic styles. Socializers often see Thinkers as overly analytical fussbudgets. Directors might sooner die than turn into dull plodders like the Relaters. Thinkers, while often drawn to Relaters, have difficulty understanding the Socializer's lack of focus or the Director's impatience. And Relaters only wish everyone was as amiable as they are.

So the potential for such conflict is always there. But the potential doesn't need to become the reality. Because, as the Relater said, they all *do* have contributions to make.

In fact, with judicious use of **The Platinum Rule**, you can not only reduce or avoid conflict, you may be able to shape some work groups into exceptionally effective tools. By understanding how groups work and how individual styles mesh or clash with one another, you can help create a whole that's much larger than the sum of its parts.

How much work time do *you* spend in meetings with at least two other people? If you're like many of us, you've got planning meetings, staff meetings, project meetings, budget meetings . . . the list seems nearly endless. No wonder one office joker described meetings as "the practical alternative to work." Some estimates are that as much as 50 to 80 percent of a manager's time, for example, is spent with groups.

Organizations love such groups; they call them teams, committees, task forces, boards, panels, whatever. And why shouldn't they? When they work well, groups can improve coordination, help employees feel more involved, and maybe even spur innovation.

But when groups flop—or, more commonly, just deteriorate into mediocrity—they can drain an organization of its vitality and leave a legacy of frustration. Posturing, power struggles, and misunderstandings are so rife that you've probably more than once wondered if more wouldn't get done if your group never met again.

SPOTTY TRACK RECORD

One of the reasons for the spotty track record of work groups is that we're generally naive about them. Too often we assume that a group can automatically be a team. We act as if we can just order a good group from Purchasing, and so we opt for an off-the-rack model instead of designing one that will best do the job.

"Round up the usual suspects," the gendarme ordered in the famous line from the movie *Casablanca*. And frequently that's what bosses seem to be thinking when they originate committees or task forces. They say something like "Hey, we'll get a few of our best minds together and figure out this problem!" Or "Let's appoint anyone who might know something about this issue." Or "Grab anybody who's got a stake in this thing."

But, in truth, making those choices is not as simple as it sounds. And whom you choose *will* very likely affect the outcome. The key is to analyze the objective before you recruit a group and then create a team that best matches the desired results.

One of the biggest single reasons that teams misfire is that personality differences are ignored. That can be the fault of the group's creator, the team members themselves, or both. In any event, that's where **The Platinum Rule** comes in. As we've learned, all people are not created equal—at least, not so far as their behavior patterns are concerned.

Knowing and taking into account those differences is what can help make the best possible use of the strengths of each team member. Directors can do some things a whole lot better than Socializers. A Thinker might easily handle something that would drive a Relater nuts.

If you're armed with **The Platinum Rule,** you'll be more able to:

- assign projects to those likely to do them well;
- sustain a cooperative climate in which each person can gain genuine respect and recognition; and
- customize work groups to get the best results in the most efficient, satisfying manner.

HOW THE FOUR STYLES ACT IN GROUPS

The four personality styles each bring different perspectives to a group, and different ways of doing things, too. First, let's take a look at some of the basic characteristics of the four styles in group situations: how they communicate, use influence, set goals, involve others, and make decisions.

Communicating

Each style of person communicates in ways so different that it's no wonder misunderstandings occur. Directors, for example, tend to communicate with short, task-oriented comments, particularly at the start of a meeting when they like to assume control and set the meeting in motion. More than the other styles, they're concerned about having a clear agenda and setting the tone. They like to keep the discussion on track and on time.

Directors usually talk most at the beginning and end of meetings, perhaps losing interest in the middle. They also may jump into a discussion, bringing lots of energy and a sense of urgency. Then they may pull back, often in frustration with the failure to make rapid, tangible progress. Before long, they begin to call attention to how much time has gone by. Soon they're pressing for closure and for concrete decisions.

Socializers, by contrast, communicate more frequently and more evenly throughout a meeting. Their comments are more likely to include jokes and to cover a range of topics so wide that the Socializers may appear to be hopping all over the place.

Relaters seem generally interested in discussions throughout the whole meeting. They may ask specific questions, trying to understand others' points of view or what follow-through will be expected. They naturally act as linking pins, go-betweens, or natural facilitators by saying things like "Now, if I understand what Jane and Tom meant, it's that the next step is to . . ." or "To get back to Samantha's comment, it seems that her idea dovetails nicely with what Bob mentioned a few minutes ago."

On the other hand, Thinkers usually just quietly observe until they fully grasp an issue and have figured out in some detail what they want to say and if they'll feel comfortable saying it. They often begin by asking a few well-chosen questions. Then, if the climate seems receptive, they'll build up to a more direct statement about what they believe is the actual answer.

Using Influence

The different styles also try to sway, or influence, the group in different ways. This can become critical because, as we'll see later in this chapter, at an early stage every group wrestles with the issue of who's going to wield power.

Directors like to influence others by structuring agendas, tasks, and assignments and, if relevant, using their formal position as leverage ("As general manager for the past eighteen years, I've seen these situations develop, and I think . . .")

Socializers are more inclined to use flattery or compliments to win over the group and get its members to feel good as a team. They'll often use humor to defuse tension or conflict. They try to avoid a hard line that will lose them acceptance or recognition by the group.

Relaters, whether they're anointed leaders or not, often take on the role of keeping the process moving along. They'll elaborate on what others say and encourage everyone to have their say. They seek to exert influence indirectly by keeping things mellow and moving.

Information and logic are the tools of the Thinkers. They like to focus on information that, directly or indirectly, suggests their expertise and experience. ("Remember, I was one of those who came up with the original plan. The rationale at that time was clear, and I think what we want to do here is . . .") They're the most likely to focus on the "rightness," or logic, of a solution rather than spending a lot of time debating who's personally helped or hindered by it.

Setting Goals

The different styles often have different goals in mind. Even the number of objectives can differ.

Directors prefer to focus on one bigger goal. Ideally, it involves an action that's also efficient, productive, and cheap. Socializers, by contrast, may have many loosely defined objectives and those may change in the course of the process. If there's a consistent theme to the Socializers' goal-setting, it's getting the job done by being nimble, by changing as much or as often as needed.

Relaters tend to favor specific goals. If they must choose just one, it would be one that opens opportunities for themselves and others to work well together. So, for example, they might favor dividing the problem into parts and then assigning subgroups to handle each part.

Quite to the contrary, Thinkers, like Directors, strongly prefer a single goal for the group. Thinkers especially like goals that put the greatest emphasis on accuracy or quality—say, deciding to produce the best item, rather than one of lesser quality that might be made more quickly or more cheaply. Thinkers also favor goals that promote the growth of something: size, profit, efficiency, customer satisfaction, or anything that can be reflected in an upward trend line.

Involving Others

Working in a group, by definition, means involving others. But there are variations in why and how enthusiastically the four styles embrace the others.

Generally, groups put together by Directors will be smaller and have shorter meetings than those set up by people with other styles. Often, the Director will want the group to make some key decisions on key issues, then delegate the rest of the work to individuals or subcommittees.

Socializers are more inclined to favor groups for groups' sake. They like others to be involved in the give-and-take. Not everyone who's put on a committee by a Socializer will have a logical role there but, in the Socializer's mind, that person is additional seasoning for the soup if not necessarily a main ingredient.

Relaters also are innately attracted to groups. However, instead of using meetings for presentation of reports, they prefer to work toward consensus as they collect information from many sources.

Thinkers, too, involve others in groups to get information from a wide variety of sources. However, the Thinkers are just less comfortable operating in groups. So they prefer to have much of the group work done behind the scenes by subgroups or individuals. The Thinker especially likes to be the only one who knows how all the parts of the group's task puzzle fit together.

Decision-Making

Last, the four styles differ in their approach to group work because they tend to make decisions differently.

In a meeting run by Directors, decisions are more likely to be made unilaterally by the Director, or he will call for a vote—especially when he knows he has the required number. Directors like voting because it's clean, quick, and decisive. It keeps debating to a minimum. Also, it's harder to argue that a vote is unfair. And closure is clearly attained. *Next* topic!

A problem with voting—though the Directors rarely see it as a problem—is that there are winners and losers. Socializers, being more people-oriented, try to work out compromises that reduce resentment and maybe even fudge over differences. Socializers want to downplay group divisions, so they're not big on voting.

Relaters also prefer decisions by consensus. They'd like to see the whole group be on the bus. So actions tend to be worked and reworked until almost all are in agreement.

Thinkers crave "rational" decisions. Optimally, the decision won't be made as much as it will be dictated by the facts and logic of the situation, including the key players required to make it work. Thinkers like to list pros and cons of issues—sometimes even weighing the options numerically—to reach the "correct" decision. The process, they believe, will make the best course of action obvious.

So all these differences make work groups trickier than they may seem at first glance. But such differences also can be used to advantage.

In modern business, it's particularly important to be alert to dissimilarities. Yesterday's management style was "my way or the highway." Today, though, consensus-building is emerging as the ultimate king, and being a good communicator isn't an option but an imperative.

Formal research and our own field experience have shown that teams succeed or fail based on how well they:

- deal with the personal styles of all team members, including their adaptability;
- match the purpose and critical tasks of the team with the strengths of its members;
- mesh with other groups in the organization.

Such internal considerations are at the heart of most team, or group, problems and opportunities.

We're now going to look at how groups can be more effective by taking advantage of personality-style differences.

But first understand there are two basic ways to set up a group to optimize the effectiveness of our individual styles: diverse teams and targeted teams.

DIVERSE TEAMS

These are groups comprised of employees from all four styles, much like the hypothetical team in our opening anecdote. Having such a mixed group is a two-edged sword.

The downside is that the Directors, for example, may be trying to bring debate to a close while Relaters or Socializers are trying to whip up more discussion and heal any rifts. But on the positive side, when such group members appreciate their own and others' styles, they much more commonly divide up tasks in such a way that everyone makes a maximum contribution.

Each behavioral style can play a special role. Thinkers are terrific analysts and real sticklers for quality. Thus they can help a group narrow its range of choices and ensure quality control. Relaters, who are naturals at cooperation, are often great facilitators. Directors can give the group structure and momentum, and Socializers may prevent conflict from becoming disabling.

Each style has strengths that can complement the weaknesses of others. The four would make an excellent team if they would all practice **The Platinum Rule**. They would likely solve broad problems better and display more creativity than would a homogeneous group, and they would surely operate more effectively than a group that's stylistically diverse but not acting out of regard for others.

When should a manager specifically try to create a diverse team? Research shows that diverse teams are most effective when:

- the situation is undefined;
- a goal has not yet been agreed upon, or accepted; or
- the task is multidimensional, requiring a variety of perspectives and talents.

For example, a bank's research may show that a large segment of the public dislikes it. Bank officials don't know if that disapproval stems from the bank's policies, the attitude of its employees, the nature of its advertisements, or even from being confused with a similarly named bank.

In such a case, having all four personality types on a task force would increase the chances of getting a fuller picture. No one has yet "bought into" a specific answer, so there is flexibility of thinking. Creating a diverse group probably would make a breakthrough in ideas and approaches more likely.

Another plus for a diverse team is that it more closely mirrors the external marketplace, including customer preferences. So if the task is, say, to develop a consumer product or service, the diverse team may reflect commercial reality better than a more tightly focused group would.

As always, there's a trade-off. A diverse team may also present a greater potential for clashes. If a member doesn't understand or appreciate others' styles, he or she may reject their views, overtly or silently. Thus the whole process can suffer. The key, of course, is practicing **The Platinum Rule** ourselves and trying to get others to do likewise.

TARGETED TEAMS

Many groups, or teams, probably do have a mixture of styles. But sometimes you can purposely create a team in which a majority of members—or maybe all—have a common style. This gives the group a distinct identity and can be an immense advantage—*if* the right style is mated with the right task.

Many business committees or groups seek a single, primary result. So in the short term, that's what they are trying to accomplish: solve the problem, fill the position, market the product, cut the costs. That's a strong argument for creating a targeted team that can best get the job done.

If, for example, the problem is to find out why Turbine No. 3 keeps breaking down, you'd probably want analytical and results-oriented team members, such as Thinkers and Directors. For each style, though, there are kinds of tasks and situations for which they're best suited.

THE PIVOTAL QUESTION

The pivotal question is, If you could only have one outcome or result, which is the most essential at this time? Is it:

1. ENSURING bottom-line results?
2. PROMOTING ideas, opportunities, or people?
3. COORDINATING with others?
4. PLANNING to meet specified expectations?

When the Key Result Is Ensuring Bottom-Line Results

Here's where you can put your Directors to work controlling situations. They're problem-solvers who focus on practical actions and opportunities.

Efficient, task-oriented, and quick, they're entrepreneurial. So they'll emphasize cost/benefit, profit/loss, and risk/reward. The team will make decisions rapidly and follow through forcefully, taking risks when necessary.

The meetings will be brisk, with a clear agenda set early on. The discussion will soon turn to issues and who is going to do what and by when. Much of the actual work will be done outside the larger group by individuals or subgroups.

Subsequent meetings will be scheduled to bring results, or at least findings, back to the main group. Then, after a relatively brief discussion, any remaining differences usually are resolved by the group leader, or by a vote.

Advantages: A targeted Director group is terrific if

there's a need for speed, especially if the task is quite clear or easily subdivided.

For example, you've got first right of refusal on a potential site for a new factory. Within thirty days you've got to measure that site against other possible locations, then make a thumbs-up/thumbs-down decision.

A group dominated by Directors would relish such a challenge. It would assign its members to investigate the options without delay, then report back for a quick decision.

Disadvantages: The Directors' emphasis on speed can also hobble the group if the problem doesn't lend itself to quick analysis. Say the property options turn out to be a lot more complicated than first thought. Maybe there are complex legal issues or environmental-impact questions involved. Then the impatient Directors might be tempted to conveniently ignore some information and make a force-fit decision. Usually, though, that won't happen if the nature of the problem is a good match with the nature of Directors.

When the Key Result Is Promoting Ideas, Opportunities, or People

The loose, informal Socializers can be a great group to bring together when you want to provide optimism, hope, and a climate of support—or just to arrange for pure fun and celebration! Unlike the Directors, they shun divisions of labor and use a lot of humor, especially if discussion stalls.

Meetings of Socializer teams "seldom follow a fixed

agenda. If an agenda has been established, it is ignored," writes our colleague, Dr. Phillip Hunsaker in his book, *The Dynamic Decision Maker*. "After starting a meeting with a specific issue or problem in mind, a [Socializer] group tends to let whatever happens just happen. Usually, this means visiting many topics in quick succession."

As a result, groups consisting of Socializers often stand out from the others by producing a great number of wide-ranging ideas.

Advantages: Such groups are well suited for problems in which the interests of many different parties must be juggled, or in which novel solutions are sought. For example, let's say your firm must come to grips with soaring health-care costs, a subject with high potential for conflict.

Being people-oriented and averse to confrontation, the Socializers will be likely to find ways to defuse tensions. They are less likely than others to get hung up on minor details or past practices. So they may be able to forge compromises, or see ways around obstacles that others are blind to.

Disadvantages: The threat, so often the case with Socializers, is that they'll become too scattered. If each member goes off in a different direction, the team will break down and productivity will suffer. So short meetings are best, with a gentle nudge about keeping to the key issues or tasks. Remember: They're best at producing ideas, not follow-through.

When the Key Result Is Coordinating with Others

Such a team can be the Relaters' equivalent of the 1927 Yankees! What they most enjoy and do best is carrying out work in an organized, collegial manner. So being in an all-Relater group with the goal of co-ordinating with others can be akin to paradise.

Both people-oriented and production-oriented, this team can exchange a lot of ideas, then pool them to come up with group solutions. Relaters seek to resolve conflicting information and different viewpoints. They keep focused on their objectives, with the main group doing most of the analysis rather than delegating it.

A unique characteristic of a Relater group, according to Dr. Hunsaker, is its tendency to comment on the group's own process while it's happening. For example, someone might say, "Ed, you've been kind of quiet on this issue. What are your thoughts?" or "Let's think for a moment about how we might go ahead from here." Other groups might do post-mortems, but only Relaters tend to monitor the on-going progress, and that helps them stay on track.

Advantages: The open, exploratory nature of a Relater team is great for creative problem-solving. These groups seem to escape much of the infighting that often dogs other teams, so it has a higher potential for cooperation and, thus, synergy. This team, then, is effective for resolving conflicts and promoting cooperation while finding ways to build upon each others' ideas.

An example: Your firm is in an older section of town with limited parking. Your outside salesmen must park on the street when they bring in their sales contracts. The salesmen end up either getting tickets or wasting a lot of time running back and forth to feed the meters. Either way, it's becoming a morale problem. Yet the company can't afford to greatly increase its parking budget.

That might be a perfect assignment for a team of Relaters. They'd be sensitive to the morale factor while not forgetting the bottom-line consideration. They have to stretch beyond old solutions and be willing to look at everything from operating shuttle buses to staggering work hours to providing bonuses for carpools or even hiring the homeless to feed the meters.

The Relaters would enjoy being actively involved in a company-wide decision that called for creative solutions affecting individual employees in a positive way.

Disadvantages: While they're good at working with people and creating ideas, Relaters sometimes have trouble getting closure. Periodic progress and time checks can help them from straying too far afield.

When the Key Result Is Planning to Meet Specified Expectations

Thinkers are natural planners, and so they're often best for team issues such as: Are certain types of business ventures worth doing or continuing? Should we change our priorities or the ways we do things? Would different approaches or actions be more effective?

A Thinker group probably will have a show-and-tell quality, with lots of information presented in a predictable way, punctuated by serious questions. The meetings will be more formally structured than they might be with the other groups and may last a long time. But Thinkers won't lurch or thrash about. Instead, they'll persist with an analysis until they pretty much know what they should do and how and when—and, usually, why!

Seldom do Thinkers vote. Instead, support just coalesces behind what's seen as the most logical, rational choice—the one with the best and most convincing support on key criteria.

Advantages: Thinkers are thorough, accurate, and detail-oriented. Let's say, for instance, you are deciding whether to add another production line at your bottling works. A Thinker team might be a natural match. They would check on the pricing of all the equipment, calculate the labor costs, compare the cost per unit produced with the likely market price, project the change in your market share, and, in short, chart all the idea's pros and cons, backing them up with facts and figures.

Disadvantages: A significant downside risk is that the analysis could degenerate into debates over smaller and smaller details until the big picture is lost. Thinkers tend to form their opinions slowly but then hang on to them stubbornly—though often keeping their view to themselves. So there's a potential for gridlock, but a wise facilitator can help move the process along.

So when putting together a team of any sort, always be clear, above all, about what it is you want to accomplish. The people—and personal styles—you select can have a major impact on how the group will likely operate and what it will achieve.

THE IMPORTANCE OF ADAPTABILITY

Yes, choosing the "right" mix of personal styles can go a long way toward creating the results you want. But more important than the employee's behavioral style per se is that person's adaptability. That's the key to an effective team, whether diverse or targeted.

So don't think in terms of merely putting, let's say, Socializers on a team that's got to juggle the politically volatile health-care issue. Instead, think of Socializers *and* others who have the flexibility and versatility to do what is necessary to get the job done.

Highly adaptable people don't think, feel, or act like prisoners of their natural behavioral styles. Instead, they use their brains as they were intended to be used—to determine what types of behavior are most appropriate in what situations. Then they behave that way themselves, or make sure someone is acting in a way that gets the job done.

Thus, a highly adaptive Director would not merely be controlling but, if the situation required, would be interacting like a Socializer, or coordinating like a Relater, or planning like a Thinker. Likewise, highly adaptive Socializers, Relaters, and Thinkers see when they need to escape their comfort zone and adapt in the interest of the group's goals. Thus, the best group is really the one with enough adaptability to address change, complexity, ambiguity, and adversity.

Unsuccessful teams are marked by less adaptable people. These team members rigidly adhere to their own natural personal styles, fearing and resisting differing ideas or approaches. Such teams tend to bog down quickly as frustration—and sometimes rancor—mount. They plow little new ground.

A major hotel chain, for example, experienced what it called "extreme frustration" with one of its executive work groups. The committee members disagreed continually. They all tried to talk at the same time, and they all frequently felt they were being railroaded by the others. Not surprisingly, many members ended up angry and often walked away without getting much done.

Upon studying the behavioral styles, though, the group learned that its frustration was predictable: They were all Directors. All had been trying to be in charge at once. Since learning about personal styles, the committee members have tried to become more adaptable. They have looked at what other styles may be helpful in different situations and have tried to bring some of those behaviors to the table.

"They still have challenges," a company spokesperson reports, "and always will," but **The Platinum Rule** has gotten them to function better as a team.

THE NATURAL CYCLE OF GROUPS

Whether targeted or diverse, adaptable or otherwise, work groups typically follow a cycle, just like the organizations that spawn them. They face predictable obstacles, rise to the occasion or fail, and, as a result, either evolve or deteriorate. Let's now look at the stages of that cycle and see how the various behavioral styles can help or hinder.

Phase One: Finding Focus

When any group forms, it first gropes to find its collective focus. It lacks a sense of purpose—what it's about, what its structure, procedures, and goals are going to be. Members of the group ask, or at least think, Is this going to be worth the effort? Is this going to be a useful team that can get things done? Or is it just another group holding yet more meetings aimed at producing one more report that nobody reads?

In addition, each member of the group seeks to define his or her individual role during this initial phase. They silently ask the questions: Do I fit in here, or am I an outsider? Am I going to be an important member of this group with real input to give, or am I just here for appearances? Is this going to waste my time?

The Thinker and Director styles can be especially helpful during this phase. They are both skilled at finding focus, one more directly than the other. It doesn't matter whether the Thinker or Director actively shapes that discussion by saying "Now, let's decide what our goals and procedures are going to be. . . ." or whether they merely guide the discussion through their questions and comments.

What does matter is that members see that the team approach, or "plan," makes sense, and that they

174

psychologically buy into the idea of moving forward together. The more complex the challenges the group faces, the more likely that it will be a Thinker, or a highly adaptive non-Thinker, who can help get the group off to a sound start. Such reasoned analysis can help clear the muddy waters. Then everyone can see clearly the benefit in moving forward together and how to do that.

Similarly, the more the group is split over its goals, or the more history of discord among members, the more likely it is that a Director will play the key role. The group may be yearning for just such a leader. It wants and needs somebody to clear the air, to get the members either to commit or to leave so that those who remain can proceed on their terms. That's a situation ready-made for the Director.

In either event, it's likely that the Directors and Thinkers, or those who can adapt to be like them, will be instrumental at this phase by giving the group the direction to move into the next stage of development.

Phase Two: Facing the Realities

This phase tends to be a stormy one. While an individual performance by a Thinker or Director may have gotten the group through Phase One, this stage requires a new "team approach." That's partly because real, external issues must begin to be addressed here, not just the team's internal dynamics.

Further, it's at this point that reality often intrudes. The group may now begin to see how difficult its task really is, how little time and resources are available, and how the group may need to settle for a half a loaf rather than a transcending triumph.

All these factors can breed personal frustration, confusion, and disillusionment. Those feelings may be widespread, but they are likely to be expressed more openly by Directors and Socializers than by their less open counterparts.

The commitment to work together is most fragile at this time. This is the moment of truth. Here it will be decided if the group moves ahead and becomes a real team. Will it tackle the real issues in meaningful ways? Or will it become mired in its own internal power struggle?

The fundamental question that must be answered: Who has—or who will have—what power? Though the group should be moving ahead to confront its task, these internal issues are likely to linger: Who's the "top dog"? Who's the real leader and who are the followers? Who stands to gain the most and who'll likely come up the loser?

The key is whether members can look beyond that to think about the good of the group. Participation, communication, and commitment to the group are critical at this stage, or the group is likely to fall apart. This is when the Socializers can often be pivotal.

They, or those who can adapt to be like them, encourage members to participate by sharing their thoughts and feelings. Their informal brand of leadership can help send out a strong, clear signal that this is a group that *can* work together and make things better for all, and that each member is important.

Many, many groups never make it past this point. They never overcome the them-versus-us mind-set. Thus, the group is cheated of the results that can occur when employees learn to work together effectively, whether in diverse or targeted groups.

In such cases, the team may continue to have "meetings" and give lip service to "working with each other," but it will not be likely to accomplish much. Instead, members will continue to collide with one another, limiting themselves as a team and as individuals. The real loser, though, is the group and its organization.

The hope, however, is that at least some group members will see the benefits to themselves and to the team of putting aside the old rivalries and frameworks. They'll quit keeping score and instead learn to work together to get through the bumps, trials, and tribulations of this second stage.

If so, such commitment eventually begins to produce breakthrough progress. Members begin to see that who's in charge is less important than who brings what know-how and attitudes to the table. If the group can reach that point, they'll have entered the next phase.

Phase Three: Coming Together

Cooperation and collaboration now become increasingly apparent. It's at this point that Relaters can give a boost to the group's evolution. Because they accommodate differing views, the Relaters, or highly adaptive team members, help meld individual differences into group synergy. By opening their hearts and heads to one another, the Relaters, or others demonstrating Relater-like behavior, blend the discordant elements into more of a single melody. The team here begins to show consistency between what it actually does and what it said it wanted to do earlier.

The group now has coalesced into a true team. There's been a shift of identity. Whereas group members previously thought primarily in terms of "me," their framework now has become "we."

Phase Four: Reaching for Stardom

The fourth and final stage is the classic "peak-performing" level that is more the exception than the rule. But, when reached, Phase Four signals that a team really is performing at its best and highest use, that it's functioning as a whole, not just as a collection of individuals.

Its members enjoy being part of the team and express that fact. They've learned how to work together. Morale is high. The group continually produces quality and quantity output and is effectively self-managing.

In the previous three stages, Director-type behavior might have been called for on key decisions. But at this stage, a controlling style isn't needed. In fact, once a group has this momentum, such a strong-handed style can be counterproductive and could even torpedo the group's progress to date. Instead, the group's decisions flow naturally from its deliberations. Differences among its members become a source of strength, not dispute.

Love 'em or hate 'em, work groups are here to stay. But while they can be high-performance vehicles, they can also be high-maintenance ones, especially in the early stages. Both the team's creator and its members need to watch the process carefully. Only a team that fully understands and savors its members' styles is likely to be genuinely productive.

Too many teams match the wrong people with the wrong job. Groups, like individuals, shouldn't be expected to be perfect. But if the teams are assigned tasks that fit their particular styles—and if members practice **The Platinum Rule**—the advantages of stylistic diversity can quickly outweigh the group's liabilities.

When using **The Platinum Rule,** the burden of communication rests with the communicator. Group members must try to address the other person's wants and needs and remain nonjudgmental. (Remember: As always with **The Platinum Rule**, we're talking about personality *differences* here, not deficiencies.)

So in the final analysis, working with groups all comes down to suspending judgment, empathizing, trying to play to people's strengths, and enriching people by adding to their natural talents. The result, despite our differences, can be magnificent!

9

♦

CREATING A HIGH-PERFORMANCE LEADERSHIP STYLE

Don, a strong Director who owns a telemarketing company, decided to reward his sales crew with an all-expense-paid cruise to the Caribbean. He was proud that his firm had done so well recently. And he was pleased with himself for being a thoughtful boss who'd come up with such a generous bonus. He announced the junket with great fanfare in a staff meeting:

> "Ladies and gentlemen! Do I have a *treat* for you! You did such a great job this past year that I've arranged for you and your spouses, or significant others, as the case may be, to take a four-day group cruise . . . on me. It leaves a month from now, on October eleventh, going to Cancun, Cozumel, and the Grand Caymans. There'll be lots of great food, nightlife, shopping, sight-seeing, you name it. I've even planned a couple of semi-

nars by top motivational speakers on the
ship itself as well as a magician to entertain
you and a dance instructor to sharpen your
footwork on those romantic, cheek-to-cheek
numbers."

Don smiled and paused for what he expected
would be a thunderous ovation. But there was none.
Instead, amid generally low-key chatter, there were
some forced smiles and even a frown or two. Then
someone mentioned a conflict with their son's soccer
team, playing that week for the regional champi-
onship. Next, a saleswoman said her father was
dying, and she wouldn't feel right being out of touch.
Others had varying degrees of enthusiasm or conflicts. Don was stunned.

After the meeting, he took aside one of the salespeople he knew best and asked, "What gives? I knock
myself out for you people, spend a lot of money I
don't have to spend arranging a free vacation in one
of the most glamorous spots of the world. And you all
look at me like I'm Typhoid Tim. How come? I'm totally baffled."

The salesman explained how the employees appreciated the gesture, they really *did*. But it would have
been wise to check first to see if most would be free
on those dates, if they liked traveling as a group, if a
cruise was their idea of a good time, and if it was,
what kinds of activities they might enjoy on the ship.
"I, for one, think magic acts are really stupid. And I
know Fred would rather have his throat cut than get
out on the dance floor," the salesman told his boss.

"Don," he continued, "we really *do* appreciate you.
You're a great boss. But we're not all *like* you. You're

a few years older than most of us and your kids are grown, so your free time's pretty much your own. Not so with many of us. Besides, you're a bit of a party animal and enjoy drinking and dancing and staying up late. Fine, but not everybody else does."

"So I screwed up by trying to be so nice, huh?"

"No. Trying to be kind to your employees is great. But you've got to remember we're not all cast from the same mold. Paying for the trip is a wonderful gesture. But paying attention to how we differ as individuals is probably more important in the long run."

"Okay," Don said with a sigh. "I see what you mean. But how come nobody ever told me this before?"

"We did, Don, we *really did.* Remember when you decided that Fridays in the office would be 'Hippie Day' and everybody should wear tie-dyed T-shirts, jeans, and Birkenstocks—like you did in your earlier years—and only a few people came to work that way? Remember when you had the soda-vending machines in the lounge replaced by mineral water and nearly had a riot on your hands? Remember the time when . . ."

AN EXTRA INGREDIENT

If Don had already been practicing **The Platinum Rule,** he would have known better. Instead of telling his employees where they were going, how they would get there, and how they would have fun, he could have been *listening.* If he'd worked with them to find the best plan, he would have gotten more of a morale payoff for his money and his employees would have felt as if they were being treated like adults.

The Platinum Rule provides that extra ingredient that leaders can use in endless ways for their firm and for themselves. Being adaptable can help managers and supervisors build bridges to their employees and make them feel valued. By learning how best to respond to their interests and concerns, their strengths and weaknesses, you can get the most from your people as well as leave them more satisfied.

A Florida sporting goods manufacturer/retailer, for example, was headed by a classic Director whom we'll call Edward. He'd inherited the fifteen-person company, but his intense, dictatorial manner had driven it to the brink of bankruptcy.

"I can't figure this out," he told a business consultant. "My salespeople aren't working; they don't know how to sell. I tell them all day long: 'Get on the phone, get on the phone.'"

The adviser first got him to examine his own style. He saw that his impatient, headstrong manner, far from motivating people, was causing many of the problems. Furthermore, once Edward learned about personal styles, he saw that many of his employees were miscast. For example, he didn't have a single Socializer in his sales force, despite that style's natural talent for meeting and persuading new people.

For two weeks, Edward worked at adapting his style, putting the right people in the right jobs, and in general spreading the word in the office about the concept of personal styles. The results were awesome. Employees, who'd never heard of the concept of personal styles, suddenly saw how they—and others—operated. Once aware of the differences, they began to see the value of those around them, even Edward. Soon they were all working more and better as a team.

"You can't believe the difference in my organization," Edward told his coach. "I've switched people around. Sales are up enormously. Everything is booming." Within a short while, Edward had not only averted bankruptcy but had begun expanding the business.

IT STARTS AT THE TOP

The key to such a turnaround is to get the leaders on board. Says business consultant Nikki Sweet, "We won't deal with a company that doesn't let us go to the top person first." But once you do, she says, the possibilities are "virtually unlimited."

Indeed, **The Platinum Rule** can have a positive effect on almost every aspect of managing. With each of the four personality types, for example, there's a different way to:

- communicate and delegate tasks to them;
- compliment and correct them; and
- motivate and counsel them.

Learning these methods can quickly make you a more sensitive, effective manager. Sensitivity and tact are constantly demanded of managers. If, as someone once said, tact is the radar of the mind, **The Platinum Rule** can be a valuable tune-up of your antenna.

WHERE DOES YOUR POWER COME FROM?

By now, you know your primary behavioral style, and you've also pinpointed your substyle, along with growth opportunities to help you deal better with tasks and people. Keep those thoughts in mind.

Meanwhile, recognize that your power to influence employees springs from two sources. First, there's "position power." That's just what it sounds like—you're the CEO, the department head, the regional sales manager, and a certain amount of power comes with that title.

But ask any CEO what happens when he tries to get a brand of ketchup changed in the employee cafeteria. Ask the department head what happens when she decides to cut back on overtime. Ask the regional sales manager what happens when he asks all the store managers to upgrade the signs in their windows. Sometimes the bosses get their way and sometimes they don't.

So even if you have a title—plus a reserved parking space and a spot in the executive dining room—you can't rely on position power alone to get you what you want. You also need "personal power."

Increasingly in recent decades, employees have gained clout. Cultural changes, more enlightened management, and trends like the impact of court decisions have combined to provide a forum for the rank-and-file to express their true emotions and be-liefs. In fact, it's now generally believed that a leader can't really lead until he or she is genuinely accepted by those who are to be led.

If the CEO, department head, or regional sales manager gets the cooperation he or she asks for, it's not just because that person has a title. It's because he or she has also gained the confidence and trust of the average employee. It's because he or she has at-tained personal power.

So position power comes from being anointed by the hierarchy. But personal power comes from earn-ing it, from developing it. Position power is a starting point for influencing people. But it's personal power that turns mere compliance into real cooperation.

GAINING PERSONAL POWER

Clearly, you need personal power to be an effective leader. But how do you earn it?

For starters, it helps to have *vision*. This involves the process of painting a compelling portrait of the future so people will be motivated to work toward it.

You also need *self-confidence*. Not self-importance or false bravado, but an inner belief in your own ability. That can help you boldly sketch your vision.

Further, you need *expertise*. If you don't have the knowledge, skills, and proven experience, no one's likely to follow you regardless of how daringly you articulate your grand plan.

But most important of all, you need to be able to:

- Communicate
- Motivate

Personal power—in essence, your skill in dealing with people—is crucial to you and your organization, and **The Platinum Rule** can be the key to winning personal power. Why? Because . . .

- If you read employees' behavioral styles and adapt to them, you'll be much more effective than the manager who can't speak their "language."
- If you make the effort to build bridges by understanding your subordinates' hopes, fears, and dreams, they'll repay you with their best efforts.
- If you support their best qualities, if you demonstrate confidence in them, your employees are going to have faith in themselves, be happier and more productive.

In short, if you honor their individuality, their *essential differences*, they'll feel like they're on a winning team and will work harder and better for you. But you must empower them rather than just seeking power over them.

You can do that by learning to listen, observe, and talk to them, and then adapting so they'll feel important, wanted. That's **The Platinum Rule** put into action. Do that, and you'll see less tension and fewer conflicts and have a more effective, motivated workforce.

MANAGING BY STYLE

Okay, you know **The Platinum Rule** and its importance. How do you apply it when dealing with your employees? Let's look at six typical managerial situations.

1. Motivating

The Situation: You're manager of a highly competitive retail operation. You've got to tell your subordinates that prices are being raised 10 percent next month. These commissioned salespeople live or die on volume. They're not going to be thrilled at the prospect of a price hike, which the competition may not meet. But it's a decision that's already been made several levels above your head; your job is to carry it out, not debate it.

You have salespeople representing each of the four basic personal styles. How would you tailor your approach to each?

Directors: Be straightforward: Here's the new price, here's why it was raised, here's how it's likely to affect us. "So," you might say to them, "let's get working on ways to overcome the downside." Remember, the Director is battle-oriented. Describe the problem and how you're going to solve it rather than getting too involved in justifying the change or detailing its probable effect on the "team."

To the degree that you can, give the Director some measure of control: perhaps an adjusted sales goal that will inspire him or her to further achievement. "You're resourceful salespeople. I don't need to tell you how to do your jobs, and it's not productive to kick around whether this price hike was a good idea. The point is: The decision's been made. And it's up to us to show what we're made of."

Stress how the price change may alter the competitive situation. And try to come up with a quick, practical plan to counter any edge this might give your rivals.

Socializers: Explain that while this price hike may make it harder to sell the product, it will also make stars of those who do.

Remind them, if true, that they're among the best salespeople on the staff; cite their awards and accomplishments. Repeat the good things others may have said to you about their work.

Explain how their status and visibility will be raised if they can keep up, or even improve, their fine sales record. "This is a rare opportunity, not a setback. Every set of eyes in the place is going to be watching us. It's our chance to shine. And we *can* do it!"

Try to get them excited about the challenge of convincing customers that because your product is so much better, it *should* cost a bit more. Explain how a simple price increase won't change the fact that this is a great place to work, with bright, talented people and some fun times amid the effort.

Relaters: Expect resistance, though typically more passive—in the form of either increased avoidance or balking questions like "What about . . .?" or "Yes, but how . . .?" The Relater is particularly cool to change, any change. But try to support his or her feelings. Tell Relaters warmly and calmly that the price hike is a function of the economics of the business. Stress that it's not going to affect the teamwork you've all developed.

"What our company stands for—and what you in particular are known for—is trust and reliability, and that's something that's *not* going to change. The company's being upfront about this price increase; it's not trying to disguise it through service charges or other window-dressing," you tell them.

All that's changing, you say, is the price. "And," you point out, "customers make their buying decisions for lots of other reasons, too, including the dependable treatment they can count on from people like you. The company, its reputation, the management structure, are all staying the same. This price hike is not a harbinger of other shifts in the firm's policies, just a simple function of increased production costs."

If it's true, tell this employee that her work is so reliable that the effect on her personally may be minimal in the long run. Promise to sit down with the Relater a few months after the new price goes into effect to see what impact it's had on her sales and commissions. And if it's had a negative effect, you'll work with her to come up with a way to remedy that.

In general, try to show Relaters that though the product price is changing, everything else is going to be status quo, and, it's hoped, the effect of the price change will be something you can manage together.

Thinkers: They aren't going to like the price increase either, but they will want to know the reasons behind it in more detail. Thinkers will hunger for the logic behind this price increase and why the price is being raised now and by this amount. They'll already be thinking about how they're going to justify the price rise to their customers.

"Here are the facts," you might say. "I wish it were otherwise, but this is what we have to deal with. So our best bet is to understand the decision and then logically figure out its ramifications as best we can. Then do our job."

Be as precise as you can. It would be helpful to prepare a written analysis of the new price versus that of your competitors. You might want to ask Thinkers to help you review and beef up a list of the key benefits they can recite to their customers while telling them about the higher price.

Thinkers will probably also want assurances that this isn't likely to happen again anytime soon. And they'll want to know the procedures if customers complain or cancel orders.

You'll do best with the Thinker by being organized, thorough, and precise in your explanation. Provide documentation, and explain as fully as you can any new procedures or expectations.

These are four different approaches to four different behavioral types. You never misled or promised anything you couldn't produce. But you did use your knowledge of **The Platinum Rule** to explain the change in a way that each type could best relate to.

You chose to leave your own comfort zone to operate within the personality framework of those employees. Thus, they could better cope with what the price change means *for them*. You probably saved yourself and the firm a good deal of disruption and discontent. And you also showed your employees you care about them.

Most employees realize that businesses go through cycles of good times and bad times. But they judge and respond for a long time to how their boss dealt with them when the going was tough. Deal with your employees with knowledge and skill related to their individual differences and you'll find that's the kind of effort that's usually repaid manyfold.

2. Complimenting

The Situation: You're the supervisor and you've been told by your boss that morale seems to be lagging. His remedy: You should make it a point to give more positive reinforcement to the troops.

You know you have employees with each of the four personal styles, each with different motivation. Feedback that pleases some may seem irrelevant, or even mildly insulting, to others. How do you match your compliments to your workers?

Directors: Cite their achievements, perhaps listing the various jobs they've had as they've risen in the ranks. Praise their productivity, their speed, their decisiveness. Tell them you admire—perhaps even envy—their focus on getting things done.

"You've accomplished a lot here. You're a person who always gets results. And you're the kind of employee for whom good enough, isn't. You're typically making a concerted effort to win, and in the process, you enable your group and organization to win, too.

That's the kind of drive I think is going to be recognized and rewarded by the top brass as time goes by."

Socializers: Pay homage to their ideas, their creativity. "You may have more ideas in a week than I have in a year!"

Tell them how well liked they are by others, that they have natural charisma and appeal with people. And can they ever be *persuasive!*

He is also such a fun person to have on the staff, you remind him, and a genuinely warm person to boot.

Relaters: Stress their cooperativeness. Emphasize, when true, the high esteem in which they're held by others, not only as a producer but as a friendly co-worker who's good for the office's social chemistry.

Praise their relationship skills. Tell them you admire their ability to get along with others and, you note, how they typically have a friendly ear for a colleague.

Tell them how consistently well they perform. Explain how you've come to depend on them, day in and day out, for quality work and for not posing problems for management. "Employees like you can make others' jobs a piece of cake!"

Mention that you personally, apart from your role as supervisor, value the Relater as a co-worker and as a person.

Thinkers: Laud the quality of their work, their thoroughness, precision, and efficiency.

Tell them you marvel at how well organized they are and how they've developed systems and processes that make things flow more smoothly and logically.

"I admire your conscientiousness and persistence, too. Once you get on a project, you're like a bulldog, digging up information and sticking with the task until it's complete. I know that when I give *you* something, it's going to be done right."

3. Counseling

The Situation: You've got four workers whose performance seems to have slipped. They appear more moody and listless than usual. You think they may be troubled by something at work or home. If each were of a different personal style, how would you best approach the subject?

Directors: Stick to the facts. Draw them out by talking about the desired results rather than analyzing the problem to death.

Then discuss their concerns, but focus on tasks more than feelings. Ask them how they would solve the problem.

"You tell me. What do you think's the best way to tackle this? I know you want to maximize your performance. You're that kind of person; you're a doer, not just a talker. And we both want you to whip this thing. So how do you suggest we go about it?"

Socializers: Allow plenty of time. They'll probably not want to approach the problem head-on.

"You're usually such a happy, on-top-of-the-world kind of person. Your great attitude is one of your real strengths. But lately you haven't seemed quite yourself to me. I just want you to know that you can confide in me, you know. Anytime. The two of us always have had a good rapport. And listening to others when needed is a big part of what I'm here for."

When the Socializer finally does get around to the dilemma, she may approach it in a manner that is understated and oblique. You'll need to listen carefully for facts and feelings and pose follow-up questions to get at the heart of the matter.

Many times Socializers merely need to get something off their chests. So just talking to a caring ear may solve the problem.

Relaters: Allow plenty of time to explore their feelings and understand the emotional side of the question. Draw them out through gentle questions and attentive listening.

Create a nonthreatening environment. "You and I have known each other for a long time. We've been through plenty of ups and downs together. I hope you know that, quite apart from our roles, I care about you and I'm here for you if there's something you want to share. If there is a problem, you know I'll work with you on it, regardless of what it is."

Thinkers: Tell them you've wondered if something is troubling them, and ask questions to help them give you the right information. Let them show you how much they know.

You might outline a procedure to deal with it. "We could meet to review things, just you and I, for, say, an hour or two each week. If that doesn't work for you, I could set up a meeting for you with another resource—perhaps in Employee Assistance or, if you'd like, outside the company. My point is, you don't have to grapple with this by yourself. There are a number of different options, if you'd like to explore them. None of them is set in stone; they're all at your doorstep. And you can make changes later if they're not working for you, and then we'll figure out a different approach."

4. Correcting

The Situation: You run Accounts Payable. Lately, there have been far too many errors. The firm has gotten complaints from customers who have been overbilled or billed twice for the same service. Your boss says this has got to stop—*now!* How are you going to draw your employees' attention to this without causing another problem?

Directors: Stress the result wanted and, as far as possible, let them come up with ways to achieve it. Set up a time for them to get back to you with a progress report.

"Our goal is to eliminate billing errors totally. If anybody can do it, we can. Let's make this a major push, and let's get started right now."

Socializers: Don't be vague. Specify exactly what the problem is and what behavior is required. Have the Socializer repeat the agreed-upon changes back to you so there's no chance of miscommunication.

"I definitely need your help on this. We're being scrutinized by the big bosses on how well we deal with this problem; our reputation as a department is at stake. So I need you to get cracking on this plan. Top priority. I'll send you a memo underscoring what we've talked about here. Any questions?"

Relaters: Focus on performance, not personality. They're sensitive, so go out of your way to explain there's nothing wrong with them personally. Also, stress empathy.

"You can understand, I'm sure, what it'd be like to pay your bill and then get another invoice saying you hadn't. Or to get two or three statements all about the same time and for the same amount. It'd be confusing, at best—and probably very annoying. We both want to keep these customers happy, so please help me in trying to eliminate these errors. We've got good employees, and I think we make a good team. But some gaps have crept into our billing procedures, and we've all got to stamp those out with follow-through improvements."

Thinkers: Be specific. Say precisely what's being done wrong and name the resources you expect will be needed to correct it.

Set a deadline for when you'd expect error-free billing and a series of steps to get there. Plan another meeting in a week or two to see how those steps are working and if midcourse corrections are needed.

"We're probably not going to lick this thing all at once. After all, the problem didn't just develop overnight. But let's get a sound remedial plan on line now—and then we can perfect it further from there."

5. Delegating

The Situation: A reorganization has placed two departments under you, and your workload has soared. You're putting in incredibly long hours—and still not getting everything done. At this rate, you may end up in Intensive Care. You've got to unload some of your tasks to subordinates. Yet there are no extra titles or money to pass out along with the extra duties. How can you best hand off some of your burden without making your people feel you're dumping this on them?

Directors: Give them the bottom line—and get the heck out of the way!

"Look, here's the situation: The reorganization has quadrupled my workload. I can't do it all; nobody could. But it's all got to be done if our department is going to continue to be a standout in this company. It's a tough thing for me to ask. But you're a can-do person, somebody who always gets results and someone I've always been able to count on when the chips were down. I really need you to come through for me on this one."

Emphasize how the added responsibilities will increase their significance to others, if that's the case. Give them parameters, guidelines, and deadlines, but then let them figure out how to best accomplish the added chores. Then don't look over their shoulders; let them come back to you with progress reports.

Socializers: Stress how taking on these new tasks can get them more attention and recognition not only from you, but probably from others as well.

"There's no money or fancy nameplate that goes with this right now. But I think it's safe to say that you'll be helping yourself in the eyes of others. Around here, people who pitch in and go that extra mile tend to get recognized. Plus, you're so bright and fun to be around and have such good social skills that getting you involved in more departmental areas won't ruffle as many feathers as it might if I gave the same assignment to some others."

But make sure you get clear agreement on what the new tasks are and how they're to be done. Establish checkpoints so that there aren't long periods of time between progress reports to you and your face-to-face or at least phone review with them.

Relaters: Make a personal appeal to their dedication. "You and I have been working here, in various capacities, for—what?—twenty-some years. You know that I've come to count on you in times of crisis. And that's exactly what we have here. I need you to help me out on this. Although there's no immediate payoff in money or position, I'll remember your help as time goes by. As I say, you and I have been around the track more than a few times, and you know I'm true to my word when I make a promise like that."

When you explain their additional tasks, go over exactly what needs to be done and how you're sure a routine can quickly be established that will minimize the added burden. State the deadlines and explain why it's important to do the tasks in a specific way.

Thinkers: Explain the logic of why you need to split your workload. Offer details about how much your work has grown as a result of the reorganization.

Give them figures showing how it's more work than is humanly possible to complete.

"I know you're already working hard yourself, and believe me, I wouldn't ask you to do this if I had any other alternative. But you're so organized and such a good planner, I concluded that you could figure out a way to accomplish these additional tasks as priority items, and perhaps do so with less trouble than some others in the office. And, most important, I know these jobs are likely to be done *right!*"

Take the time to answer all Thinkers' questions about structure and the kind of guidance they might require. The more they understand the details and the more predictable the tasks are, the more likely that the Thinker will see the extra work as do-able, perhaps even a growth or learning opportunity. Be sure to establish deadlines and clarify limits.

6. Developing Talent

In addition to using **The Platinum Rule** to get maximum performance from your employees, you, as a leader, also have to ask: What am I doing for *them*? How, for their sake and that of the firm, can I help them grow?

You need to be attuned to your co-workers' potential. You must help them develop into the best employees—and in doing so, even better human beings.

How to Develop Directors

Your Directors can be among your greatest assets if you can give them opportunities and avoid being threatened by their strong personalities. Don't get frustrated and write them off if you can't develop a warm relationship with them; they're into power and results, not warmth. Let them do their own thing as much as you can, and they'll repay you with awesome energy and effort.

When training a Director, what you'll probably hear him or her saying—if you listen well—is, "Make this short and direct. Just hit the high points." They aren't going to want to be bothered with a lot of details. Help them find shortcuts and streamline the routine so he or she can get results more quickly and efficiently.

If you were trying to teach them use of a new computer, for example, you might say, "Here are the five basic steps needed to get into the files, make your changes, and then get out again. You're a quick study, so you'll probably want to learn the rest on your own. Oh, here's the manual, in case you get stuck. Let me know if you need more help."

On any project, be prepared to listen to Directors' suggestions. For instance, they'll probably want to tell you what they think of the options and the probable outcomes.

When you suggest a different idea or action, be sure to point out that you're trying to work in ways that are acceptable to both of you. "Charlotte, I understand where you're coming from when you say you want to finish the Shipley project by this afternoon. But I know that you, like me, would rather be right than quick. What if you had the rough draft in to me by, say, four-thirty? That'd give me time to look it over and sleep on it overnight. Then, if we're still on track, we'll send it out tomorrow. That way we won't have lost much time but with both of us having reviewed it, we'll have ensured that it'll get the results we both want."

So, in short, you've got to be cordial but strong to deal effectively with Directors. On the organizational chart, they may not be your equal. But in their minds, they're more like your peer than your subordinate.

Shrug that off, if you can, and play to their strengths: drive, decisiveness, and force of personality. And try to help them by nudging them toward:

- being more careful and patient before making decisions or reaching conclusions;
- recognizing the contributions of others and sharing the glory; and
- paying more attention to the feelings of their co-workers and *their* contribution to results.

How to Develop Socializers

Socializers bear watching. If given too long a leash, they may procrastinate, spread themselves too thin, fail to follow up, or get sloppy with details. But if you can channel their enthusiasm with tactful reminders and hands-on help, Socializers can generate endless ideas and lend a zest to the office that's priceless.

When coaching Socializers, what you'll probably see is a desire to jump right in before they're fully prepared. Allow them to get involved. But remember their penchant for applause. So help them save face if they do something wrong and be sure to heap on the compliments if they succeed.

Probably the best single thing you can do for Socializers is to help them sort out priorities. When they find themselves surrounded by multiple opportunities, they sometimes become disoriented.

You can lessen their anxiety by stepping in and lending some structure: "I'll need the Stevenson report by Monday. If that means putting off the Shepherd case, that's okay, as long as I get that before the seventeenth. Do you understand?"

Socializers are dreamers. They're less motivated by facts or issues than concepts. Try to support that trait by carving out time for the two of you to get to know each other better and toss around ideas. The Socializer will have plenty of them, and your role will be to translate creative expressiveness into practical action!

Also, if you can do so sincerely, cater to the Socializers' fathomless need for appreciation and recognition. That can improve their work and keep their morale at its usual high level.

You can further foster their growth by:

- ensuring that they see tasks through to completion;
- insisting that deadlines be met; and
- having them write things down.

How to Develop Relaters

You'll like Relaters and find them easy to work with—*everybody* does. But your biggest challenge will be to get them to break out of their ruts. They loathe change and often cling to outdated ways of doing things. Directors and Socializers sometimes can help them find shortcuts, and even a Thinker may have suggestions, if asked.

Relaters, when in training for a job, favor slower, hands-on coaching by a warm, patient human being. While a Director or Thinker might be satisfied with a manual and time to digest it, the Relater prefers an instructor who'll help him or her find comfort with each step. Relaters may want to observe others for a longer-than-average time before trying the task themselves. Only when their confidence builds will they comfortably begin.

When you have occasion to reward Relaters, do so in a personalized and low-key way because they're often uneasy with public praise. Stress how much you appreciate their efforts to make things better for you and others.

Though they often do have good ideas, Relaters may be reluctant to bring them up because they don't like the limelight. So you might want to pave the way for them a bit by saying, "Please let me know what you think of the proposed new compensation plan. It's a bit of a change, and we want it to be fully understood and, hopefully, accepted by everybody before we proceed. Your input is especially important because of all the thought you give to such things."

In most cases, expect to do more talking than listening with Relaters. They'll expect you to carry the conversational ball. Because Relaters crave clarity and stability, it's a good idea to take items, or steps, one at a time. As you complete each item on an agenda, for example, you might double-check that the two of you fully understand. "So you'll handle the Dobson account, and I'll make the preliminary checks with the lawyers on the Acme case. Is that agreed?"

Other steps you can take to promote growth in Relaters:

- Try to help them think for themselves by modifying their tendency to do what others tell them.
- Make them feel sincerely appreciated.
- When you see positive changes, get them to accept credit and praise.

How to Develop Thinkers

Thinkers, the most complex of the four styles, are often the hardest to get a handle on. But if you make the effort and do so, you'll have an employee whose diligence and quality work can make him or her invaluable.

Thinkers want to make rational choices, not decide something based on hunches or what others say or think. So when they say "Give me some time to think it over," do so within the limits that exist.

You'll have to be more on your toes when speaking to Thinkers than with any other types. They're likely to ask a lot of questions, and if they sense you're unprepared, they may lose confidence in you. Avoid exaggeration and vagueness when you speak to them because they often dissect remarks to decide if you have serious ideas worthy of serious consideration. If you come across as half-cocked, real communication may grind to a halt.

They're also very sensitive to criticism. So if you

ask questions of them, be oblique and nonjudgmental: "Sam, what are your thoughts about the deadline on the Thompson matter? Are there special problems you're encountering that I should know about?" That's far preferable to the harsher "Why is the Thompson account so late?"

When coaching Thinkers, it's best to focus on the most important things first and then proceed in an efficient, logical manner. Proceed at their pace, stopping at intervals to ask for their input and for a sense of how well they're comprehending.

That's because they like to do things bit by bit. So, if possible, let them complete a task in steps, reporting back to you at each milestone.

Other ways to help Thinkers:

- Gently request that they share their knowledge and expertise with others.
- Make sure their view is represented (preferably by themselves) with those people they'd prefer to avoid.
- Get them to make more time for people and for fun.

THE "BEST" LEADERSHIP STYLE

Remember, the best leader isn't someone with a particular behavioral style, or even some ideal blend of styles. Instead, the best leader is someone who realizes what a job or task requires—and then *achieves it!* That means working well with others. And *that*, in turn, means dealing well with *all* of the personal styles in *all* sorts of situations.

In fact, as firms re-restructure and put new emphasis on teamwork, business leaders who understand behavioral styles will have a leg up. Sometimes they may wish to act in their natural style, using their intrinsic strengths. At other times they may choose to adapt to others, using **The Platinum Rule** principles. Or, when they sense a serious clash of styles, they may wish to pick a third person to handle a certain situation.

Yet another option open to the manager is to change the work environment—say, realign a worker's duties, alter deadlines, or revamp priorities—to capitalize on employee strengths. Most managers today agree that you can't mandate productivity.

A friend of ours, for example, employed a strong Thinker as bookkeeper/office manager. She was terrific at that job, but when the boss had to leave the office, the Thinker also had to answer the phone, and that's where the trouble began. Complaint after complaint piled up about the bookkeeper's brusqueness. Finally, her boss phoned in, simulating being a customer, and was shocked at how abruptly she was treated.

"I just hate it when customers call," the bookkeeper later conceded. "They interrupt what I'm doing." Though a good worker, she wasn't cut out to deal with customer service. Needless to say, the boss got somebody else to answer the phone, and everybody was happier—the boss, the bookkeeper, and the customers!

For any organization to run the best it can, you need all four styles. You can't just say "We're a sales organization, so we need all Socializers." You need all four, and you need them in the right spots.

In all cases, though, you, the manager, should be very aware of your own style and how it can affect others. Being conscious of the extremes of your own personal style may allow you to become a better boss. Often, supervisors who make a study of their style in the workplace also see improved relationships at home and in social settings. "Wow!" they'll say as they see for the first time how others view them, "that's what my wife (or husband) has been telling me all these years."

In either case, you can choose to make *your* style more palatable. Here, then, is a quick summary of what a manager can do to round off some of the sharper edges of his or her personal style:

When You're a Director . . .

Ratchet down a notch or two. Keep in mind that others have feelings and that your hard-charging, know-it-all style can make your subordinates feel inadequate and often resentful.

Accept that mistakes *will* occur, and try to temper your passion with compassion. You might even joke about errors you make, rather than trying always to project a superhuman image.

Directors can encourage growth in others in at least two ways. One, by praising them when they do something well. Secondly, by giving them some authority and then staying out of their way so they can use it. Whatever you lose in control you're likely to gain in commitment and improved staff competency.

Try not to be quite so bossy! Ask others' opinions and maybe—though this is *radical* for a Director—even plan some collaborative actions.

When You're a Socializer . . .

Your people depend on you not just for ideas, but for coordination, too. So anything you can do to become more organized—making lists, keeping your calendar current, prioritizing goals—can pay big dividends for you *and* them.

Nothing's so dispiriting as to see the boss drop the ball on important matters. So remember: If you fail to follow up, if you procrastinate on tough decisions, if you don't stay current with new "know-how" and key details, or if you make pledges you don't keep, your employees will lose faith. Even though you don't do those things purposely, they'll see you as letting them down. Your charm and warmth can't fully compensate for unreliability.

Also, come to grips with the fact that conflicts are going to occur. Try to deal with them upfront, not sweep them under the rug. In addition, organize your priorities—and then your time—to keep your social talents in balance with your contributions to tasks.

When You're a Relater . . .

You're probably a well-liked boss. Your goal should be to become a more *effective* and still well-liked boss.

Learn to stretch a little, taking on more, or different, duties and trying to accomplish them more quickly. You may benefit by being more assertive at times as well as more open about your thoughts and feelings. Experiment with a little risk, a little change.

Being sensitive to your employees' feelings is one of your greatest strengths. But you must seek a middle ground between that and being knocked off balance by the first negative comment or action that comes your way.

When You're a Thinker . . .

Your high standards are a two-edged sword. Your employees are inspired by your quest for excellence, but often they feel frustrated because they can never quite seem to please you.

One of the best things you can do is lessen and soften your criticism, spoken or unspoken. You can seem so serious and intense sometimes!

Ease up on your need for process control. Take five minutes a day to walk around and spend more time with the various players, making friendly contact with people at the watercooler or in the lunchroom.

Wake up to the fact that you can have high standards without requiring unnecessary perfection in each instance. That will take a load off your shoulders—and off your employees, too.

10

♦

HOW TO SELL BY STYLE

Carla is a computer salesperson and a darn good one, she thinks. She speaks the language, rattling off "gigabyte," "random access memory," and "microprocessor" as if she learned the terms at her mother's knee. She knows her inventory, too, and she makes it a point always to dress smartly, smile broadly, and look the customer right in the eye.

So why is it that Carla doesn't *sell* much?

Well, let's take a look:

> A man in his early thirties is browsing through the display of printers. Carla approaches, introduces herself, and starts to tell the customer about that particular model: How many pages per minute it cranks out, what fonts it contains, how it can be upgraded to a larger memory at only a nominal cost.
>
> The customer flips through some notes

he's brought with him and asks Carla if this printer does envelopes. Carla says it does pretty much everything and goes on to say that a company down the street bought four of them yesterday.

The customer asks about producing letterheads. Carla tells him the machine's print quality is excellent and, in fact, this model has been endorsed by a leading computer magazine.

The customer asks if it can print labels. Carla says there is "almost nothing this little gem can't do. It's attractive, too. Looks good in any office."

The customer puts away his notes, thanks Carla for her time, and leaves. Carla shakes her head. "Some people are just hard to sell to," she mutters to herself.

What did Carla do wrong? From the point of view of **The Platinum Rule,** almost everything. She made assumptions about what her customer wanted. She didn't ask questions, and she didn't really listen to the customer's questions. She presumed that the customer would be interested in what Carla was interested in.

She didn't learn the first thing about the customer's wants and needs, let alone respond to them. Instead, Carla tried to fit the customer into a sales mold. She should have been trying to fit her sales style to the customer. But because she didn't, she lost the sale.

FEELING UNDERSTOOD

In truth, customers don't buy because they're made to understand the product or service. They buy when *they feel understood*.

So the successful salesperson shows customers that he or she understands them by giving them what they expect, or *more*. But more what?

That's where **The Platinum Rule** comes in. Now that you understand its principles, you know that the "more" can vary. For the Director customer, it's more *control*. But the Socializer cries out for more recognition and *excitement*. The Relater wants more *support*, and the Thinker more *logic*. The best salespeople customize their approach and follow-through. This chapter will show you how to deal with each of the four styles at each step in the business relationship.

But there's more to sales than just viewing each customer through the prism of personal styles. The best salespeople also reject the traditional concept of a sale. They realize that the world has changed in significant ways and that salespeople today need new skills, new attitudes, and a new understanding of how to work with their clients.

Selling systems of the past won't work today because they were designed to work in an adversarial environment. But when your customers are your partners—and you want them as *lifetime* partners—you can't sell using commando tactics. An adversarial relationship just won't work.

Instead, the modern, collaborative salesperson helps the customer solve a problem, fill a need, or reach a goal. He doesn't see the sale as just a one-time event in which persuasiveness triumphs over resistance. Rather, he views it as a cooperative triumph that paves the way for a long-term partnership.

That's because today's customers aren't looking for quick fixes. They're looking for long-term relationships with suppliers who will be resources for them over the long haul. Thus, your ability to collaborate with your customers will make or break your career.

So selling effectively today means better handling of the interpersonal aspects of a sale in order to build a strong base of lifetime customers. Now we'll look at ways to best cement that relationship, regardless of the customer's style.

A GOLDEN KEY

Salespeople who practice **The Platinum Rule** as well as this collaborative approach to sales will find that the benefits cut both ways. Their customers will regard them not as just another hawker, but as a valued, trusted resource. As a result, the salesperson's sense of professionalism and self-esteem will rise. Which, in turn, will translate into satisfied relationships, more sales, and a greater sense of self-worth.

Take the case of a guy we know who started selling Toyotas in the early 1980s. He was so laid-back, so people-oriented, so lacking in the customary intensity, that his peers in the showroom actually made fun of him. For one thing, they thought he was off the wall with his emphasis on getting customers whatever fact they wanted, no matter how long it took or how difficult it was to get. Secondly, he absolutely refused to pressure people. "The coconut will drop from the tree when, and if, it's ready," he once said. The others tittered.

But, before long, unusual things started happening in that showroom. Some of his customers began coming by just to chat and say how they were enjoying their car. New prospects would ask for him by name because of referrals. He was named Salesperson of the Month so many times that he ran out of wall space to hold all his plaques. As his more competitive colleagues looked on in amazement, he was named sales manager of the dealership.

Then one day he was gone. He was recruited by corporate headquarters to teach others about effective selling. Not bad for the guy the others used to poke fun at.

That's the kind of success collaborative selling, combined with **The Platinum Rule,** can bring about. The head of a financial-services firm who taught these concepts to his sales force described the result to us this way: "My entire company is using your techniques with tremendous success. . . . It is just as easy as having a golden key to unlock each prospect's mind."

The key metaphor fits because sales is a matching process. You match: (1) the right product or service to your customer's needs; (2) your customer's buying pace with your selling pace; and (3) your customer's buying style with your selling style.

To do so, you must learn to adapt your style to that of your customer. That's what Carla didn't know. That's **The Platinum Rule.**

HOW YOU PERFORM

Whatever your business, there are five steps to making a successful sale. Each personal style needs to be handled a little differently at every point along the way, and we'll examine those approaches.

But first, let's take a broader look at how *you* likely perform as a salesperson, depending upon your behavioral style, and similarly, how your clients or customers usually behave, based on their styles.

The Director

As a Salesperson: You move rapidly into a presentation and give the customer the bottom-line benefit. You've got just one objective in mind, so you prefer to dispense with small talk unless you sense it's essential. If a prospect doesn't see the benefits, you may lose patience and move on to your next prospect.

You're confident, so you paint convincing pictures of the benefits of your product or service. You tend to have a higher tolerance for rejection than the other styles, so you're comfortable with cold calls.

Your quick pace and bottom-line orientation mean you are wired to do well selling products that can be quickly matched to a customer's needs. Examples are investments, cars, or insurance. Your impatience makes you less well suited to products or services requiring lengthy customization. Those might include complex computer services, communication systems, consulting projects, and other services with long sales cycles.

As a Customer or Client: Directors make decisions quickly based on facts and data. But they become bored with presentations that are too technically detailed. They want to know: *What* will this product do for *me*? not, How does it work?

They prefer salespeople to get to the point and offer solutions that will provide the results they want. Directors also expect you to look and act professionally.

As customers, Directors seek to maintain control of the sales process. They won't want to meet with you a second time if they can help it. So it's important to get them information as soon as possible and not oversell them or waste their time.

They don't want to develop a personal relationship with salespeople. But they do want to have confidence in them, their information, and their product.

They also like having options. So you can streamline their decision-making by laying out the choices and backing each one up with evidence. It's important to be prepared for each encounter with a Director customer.

When selling to Directors, also keep in mind that they:

- think in practical terms, not theoretical;
- welcome changes and new opportunities;
- have a fear of being hustled;
- put low priority on feelings, attitudes, and opinions; and
- are cool, independent, and competitive.

The Socializer

As a Salesperson: Your enthusiasm, optimism, and attraction to people give you a leg up in most sales situations.

You do best when you deal with a lot of prospects briefly rather than enduring protracted analyses or negotiations. So you are likely to do well in areas such as real estate, automobiles, media (especially fast-paced radio and TV), and health-club memberships.

You like sales jobs that give you a lot of freedom and provide variety and fun. You excel when you can sell emotional benefits (such as prestige, class, uniqueness) as part of the solution. You're good at selling the sizzle of vanity, so you like offering products or services that help your customers look good: cars, clothes, beauty services, yachts, art, and jewelry.

You take the time to learn your customers' likes and dislikes and selective details—birthdays, kids' names, vacation habits—that personalize your dealings. You naturally seek ways to connect with your customers, and your friendly, open nature is a great asset.

As a Customer or Client: Socializers like to be sold emotionally, not logically. So a good salesperson will show a Socializer how a product or service will make her stand out and enable her or others to feel good—personally or professionally.

They often make decisions based on impulse or first impressions. They think the sales process should be fun, and they like lunches, golf, and other social events that often accompany selling. Socializers need to be liked, so they may want to be treated like a friend before being sold.

They abhor paperwork, so the sales process ought to be simple and easy. After they say yes, everything should happen smoothly, without their involvement.

They are "whole picture" people who enjoy being given a range of several appealing possibilities. An effective salesperson can help Socializers narrow their choices and focus on a solution.

When selling to a Socializer, also keep in mind that they:

- dislike conflict;
- don't respond well to an aggressive close;
- thrive on enthusiasm;
- are concerned with appearances and approval; and
- like change and innovation.

The Relater

As a Salesperson: You have many pluses as a salesperson. Your natural style is to build relationships and to progress slowly through the sales process. You enjoy listening to your customers' needs, and you sincerely want the best solutions for them.

You're best at dealing with a few prospects over a longer sales cycle. You also enjoy sales that require a team approach.

You seldom push for a close because you're not comfortable doing so—and because you don't think you *need* to. Because you're so thorough and patient, you expect the customer to commit when ready as a natural part of the sales process.

As a Customer or Client: Relaters want to be able to depend on a salesperson before making a purchase. They're rarely in a hurry and are turned off by intense, overbearing salespeople. They respond well to lower-key, friendly attention. They want salespeople who listen and are sensitive to their buying needs.

Once they've established such a relationship, they're loyal customers who are less likely to go elsewhere, even in the face of stiff competition.

They may even bring family or co-workers along because they want everyone affected by the purchase to have a say.

If a Relater isn't interested in your product or service, he may find it difficult to say no. In that case, Relaters may invent excuses or insist on delays in order to escape.

When selling to Relaters, remember also that they:

- have a low tolerance for conflict;
- avoid risk or change when possible;
- need to know what to expect, step-by-step;
- like time to think things over; and
- need to know they will be supported.

The Thinker

As a Salesperson: You're current at providing the prospect with lots of key information. You're not particularly relationship-oriented, so you do best when you can appeal to a customer's intellect or "factual" and "logical" considerations in buying products.

You'd work well with professional and technical types of buyers. That's because when you sell to them, you can focus on your highly organized, logical presentation of data and rationale.

You take the time to understand your customers' needs as well as the use they have for your product or service. It's easy for you to analyze the logic of their situation and make a good recommendation backed up by hard data. You prefer that to selling on the basis of "softer," more subjective, personal interests.

As a Customer or Client: The task-oriented Thinkers want detailed information about how your product or service will fill their specific needs, and they want time to study and verify that data. They respond well to graphs and charts.

Sometimes they may become intrigued to the point of seeming obsessed with nonessential details. So you can help them make decisions more quickly by drawing their attention back to the big picture, stressing the comparative key features and benefits of your product or service for their situation.

Thinkers want to lower their risk when buying. So anything you can offer them along those lines—guarantees, free trials, pilot programs—may help clinch the sale. They want salespeople to be, above all, knowledgeable. They're turned off by those who seem too direct or too enthusiastic.

Somewhat formal, they don't want or need to spend a lot of time chatting with salespeople. A few short phone calls, for example, might work better than a series of time-consuming meetings.

When selling to Thinkers, don't forget that they:

- need to understand how things work;
- enjoy the process of problem-solving (on their own terms);

- like to be admired for their accuracy;
- prefer to accomplish tasks by themselves; and
- want to avoid conflict, debate, and embarrassment.

ADJUSTING PACE AND PRIORITY

Once you figure out the behavioral style of your customer, you can adapt and build rapport. As we saw in Chapter 7, the first adjustments to make involve our pace and priority.

You can get rid of much tension in a relationship if you start by simply adjusting your *speed* of doing things. Then alter, if need be, your priority—that is, whether you emphasize *task* or *relationship*.

If you are a direct person (Director or Socializer) and you want to deal better with indirect customers or clients, remember that they make decisions more slowly and more privately, so first be more relaxed. Ask their opinions and find ways to acknowledge and incorporate their opinion in the dialogue. Follow their lead rather than seeking control in ways that increase their tension, and thus resistance.

Make it a point to listen more than you speak, and when you do speak, don't interrupt, challenge, or push the process along faster than they want it to go. Be more subtle about any disagreement.

If you're an indirect person (Relater or Thinker) selling to a direct person, you need to pick up the pace. Initiate conversations, give recommendations, avoid beating around the bush. Maintain eye contact, use your firmest handshake, speak strongly and confidently.

As for priority, if you're an open person (Relater or Socializer), you naturally emphasize relationships and feelings. But to deal best with more guarded customers, you'll want to put more emphasis on the task. So get right to it: Talk about the bottom line, use facts, logic, and documented proof of results. If possible, prepare an agenda of key points and stick to it. Keep your meeting focused and short.

Downplay your natural warmth; guarded people view excessive friendliness as "put on." They also don't like to be touched by strangers or have their physical space invaded. So don't make further physical contact—beyond a handshake—until you're sure it's likely to be well received.

Conversely, if you're guarded (Director or Thinker), put the relationship first when dealing with open people. Share your feelings, and let them know more about you as a person. Show an interest in them: their job, family, hobbies, for example. And then use that knowledge in the future to personalize your dealings with them.

Slow down and talk more. Try to speak in a friendly, informal way. Be flexible with your time, tolerating digressions such as stories and anecdotes.

Open people are more comfortable with closer proximity. So stand closer than you normally might. Use a few relaxed gestures such as leaning back, smiling, or gently patting the customer on the back or shoulder.

The point is: *Everybody is easy to please, if you know how.* With Directors, be efficient and competent. With Socializers, listen and support their ideas or dreams and flatter them. With Relaters, stress your warmth and sincerity, and for Thinkers, take care to be especially thorough and well prepared.

FIVE STEPS TO SALES SUCCESS

Once you've identified a qualified prospect, there are five steps, or phases, to any successful selling process. (These steps are taken from *Collaborative Selling*, by Alessandra and Barrera.) You can learn to adapt at each step, depending on which of the four basic personal styles we're dealing with.

The five steps are:

1. *Contact.* Showing the prospect that you have his or her best interest at heart and setting the stage for the rest of the process to continue smoothly.
2. *Explore.* Studying your prospect's situation to uncover needs that you can fill.
3. *Collaborate.* Involving your customer in determining the best solution.
4. *Commit.* Getting to "Yes." Traditionally, this has been known as "closing" the sale or "asking for the business." But for the collaborative salesperson who practices **The Platinum Rule,** this stage is often just a formality. If there's been mutual agreement up to this point, the Commit stage is just the culmination.
5. *Assure.* Keeping in touch after the sale. This is the secret to long-term success. It's here that you make sure the customer receives everything that

was promised, such as delivery, installation, and service.

Now let's look at how you can build rapport at each stage.

1. The "Contact" Stage

Making contact with your prospect is the first critical test. Your knowledge of **The Platinum Rule** will have an impact on the impression you give here. In the first few minutes, you often make, or break, the sale. In that time, your prospect sizes you up and decides if you're the type of person he'd like to do business with.

This contact may be in person, over the phone, or by letter. Each makes a different impression and has its advantages and disadvantages. In person meetings, for example, make the strongest impressions, but they are time-consuming and costly. And guarded types (Director and Thinker) may prefer a less personal introduction.

But the key, regardless of the personality type you're dealing with, is for you to "read" your client and adapt in a way that builds credibility and trust. When prospects sense you have their best interests in mind, the rest of the sales process should follow more easily.

Why should a prospect meet with you? Usually, he or she doesn't know who you are and may not even be familiar with your firm or your product. So you need to be able to convey quickly who you are and how you might be able to help.

You do this through a "competitive-advantage statement." It's a thirty-second statement that covers:

- Your name
- Your company
- A statement about a problem in the market
- How you and your product solve that problem

For example: "My name is Marlene, and I work with a company called The Prescription for Doctors. Physicians today are being pressured by insurers, patients, and employers to cut health-care costs. Yet overhead for physicians is constantly rising. We provide a service that allows the physician to spend more time with patients and cut overhead at the same time, resulting in better-quality care at a lower cost. It's just what the doctor ordered!"

Many customers are interested in cost and features. But *all* customers, regardless of their behavioral styles, want to know what benefits and value they'll receive. There's one thing everyone wants to know: "What will it do for me?"

So the competitive-advantage statement immediately answers that question and gives them a reason to talk to you. Further, you build trust by stating upfront what you're all about rather than waiting until you're halfway through the sales process.

The contact stage is pivotal. Apart from product knowledge, no other facet of the sales process makes a greater impression on the customer. And by using a competitive-advantage statement and your knowledge of **The Platinum Rule,** you can immediately set yourself apart from the competition.

So with that in mind, let's look briefly at how to

handle the "Contact" stage with each of the four personality types.

Making Contact with Directors

Directors, as you now know, are primarily concerned with the bottom-line impact of your product or service. Give them enough information to understand overall performance.

But they don't want or need a nuts-and-bolts description of your product's innards. Neither do they want to be your buddy. Nor will they decide on the basis of testimonials from your legion of satisfied customers. They just want the *facts!*

So talk about results, increased efficiency, time saved, return on investment, profits, and how your product or service will allow them to achieve their goals. In short, tell them what's in it for them.

Remember: They're impatient with slower-paced people. So move at a relatively fast pace, be well organized and time-conscious. You might approach them by saying something like "If you can give me ten minutes, I'll show you how you can improve your office's efficiency and save you both time and money."

Directors pride themselves on being busy. So they're very interested in saving time if it will allow them to accomplish their goals in the long run.

Making Contact with Socializers

In your initial contact, emphasize those aspects of your product or service that will give Socializers status, recognition, excitement, and the thrill of being the first on their block to have the "newest," "best," or "most prestigious" item available. Unlike the Director, the Socializer *would* like to be your buddy.

So you might say something like "I'd like to come by and show you an exciting new product that can effortlessly and quickly organize your accounts and help you become even more of a top producer."

When you meet Socializers, visualize acting like a politician running for election. Introduce yourself with confidence and enthusiasm. Be an especially empathic and upbeat listener. Show interest in *them*. When you talk about yourself, remember to use *feeling* words, not *thinking* words. Tell stories about yourself, too, especially humorous or unusual ones. Let them set the pace and direction of the meeting.

MAKING CONTACT WITH RELATERS

Act professional, but in a nonthreatening, pleasant, friendly manner. Listen patiently. Show your sincere interest in them as individuals and try to become their friend.

It helps to mention the name of the person who referred you, if appropriate. That's because Relaters, more than any of the other styles, prefer to do business with people they know, like, and have confidence in.

Relaters need to know what to expect. "Could I come by sometime to lay this out for you?" you might ask. "I can show you why it's an almost risk-free way to build more business. And we guarantee you'll have a service rep assigned to you and available twenty-four hours a day."

Making Contact with Thinkers

You must do your homework. You must also prove—in writing, if possible—your product's quality, track record, and value.

Avoid the hard sell. Thinkers go about tasks more slowly and dislike being rushed. Build credibility by telling them what you think, not what you feel. Speak slowly. Economize on words.

Go easy on the small talk. Thinkers tend to be cautious and therefore are naturally skeptical about people, *especially* salespeople who oversell themselves.

Your approach might be along the lines of: "I have some information I'd like you to take a look at. What it shows—in a very straightforward, factual way—is that there's a clear trend toward computer-oriented graphics in your industry. As you can see by this analysis, our researchers have made a thorough study of this, and their conclusion, backed by the numbers, is that your firm could increase its profits twenty to thirty percent over two years if you put this new program into place."

2. The "Explore" Stage

Each prospect has a unique situation that must be explored before you can discuss a solution. This may require repeated visits and research by you. Naturally, the bigger the ticket on the item, the longer and more involved this stage may be.

What you want to look for are the prospect's *problems* and *opportunities*. The problem, or need, is the gap between what a customer wants and what he or she now has. This gap already exists.

An opportunity, on the other hand, is something extra that can be added. For example, a new market, or a better avenue of distribution, or an untapped promotional vehicle. A resourceful salesperson can create an opportunity.

Thus, the purpose of the Explore stage is to get information—enough information to know the customer's needs and what it'll take to fulfill them. To do that, you need to listen to what the prospect says, but you also need to know how to ask questions.

You don't need to ask a lot of questions, just the right ones. Asking the right questions is akin to painting a picture. You start with a blank canvas and begin to fill in the background and rough in the picture with broad brushstrokes. Then you fill in the details using finer and finer strokes.

For example, remember Carla, our computer salesperson? Perhaps she's talking to a prospect who's a management consultant and is trying to persuade him to move up to a more powerful computer. The consultant says he really isn't ready to do that because business remains a bit slow and he doesn't yet really have the volume to justify a bigger computer for billing and other office chores.

Carla starts out with questions that provide information but also show her interest in the prospect's situation and help him relax. These question often start with "Tell me," "How," "What," or "Why." They are much more powerful than closed-ended questions requiring a simple yes or no or a specific bit of information.

Then she builds to more narrowly focused questions ("What aspects of your marketing could use the most help?" "Which is more important: speed, quality, or cost?")

Carla soon figures out that the consultant isn't soliciting clients aggressively enough. She shows him how, with a bigger computer and some new software, the consultant could easily do large, targeted mailings, a newsletter, automatic follow-up letters, or other target marketing that's likely to build his business.

Carla, by uncovering the customer's opportunity, becomes a consultant herself. She begins building a relationship with this customer, and when his business grows as a result of Carla's suggestion, he's likely to be back.

So, again, in the Explore stage, look for needs and opportunities. You do that by asking questions and listening. These are critical sales skills. The questioning must move at a pace that's comfortable for the prospects, and that, of course, brings us to the personal styles.

THE "EXPLORE" STAGE WITH DIRECTORS

To head off their impatience, keep your fact-gathering interesting by alternately asking questions and giving information. Make your questions as practical and logical as possible, and never ask for data that's available elsewhere.

Be well organized, time-conscious, efficient, and businesslike. Ask questions that show you've done your homework. Know the industry and the company. Be sure to ask questions that allow the Directors a chance to talk about their business goals.

Be sure to fine-tune your questions as much as possible. Aim them precisely at the heart of the issue and ask them in a straightforward manner. That's because Directors have to see the meetings as purposeful, and they want to be able to see where you are going with your questioning.

THE "EXPLORE" STAGE WITH SOCIALIZERS

Socializers get bored quickly when they're not doing the talking. So much of the information-gathering needs to revolve around them.

You can strike a balance, though, between listening to their life stories and gleaning the necessary information. When asking business-oriented questions, keep them brief and, if you can, work them into a mixture of business and social questions.

For example, you might say, "You mentioned people as being one of the keys to your success. How do you recruit the people you work with? What kind of training do you give them?"

The more you get to know your Socializer prospects, the more willing they'll be to focus on the business at hand.

The "Explore" Stage with Relaters

They're excellent interviewees if you talk warmly, informally, and ask gentle, open-ended questions that draw them out. Be tactful and sincere.

Remember, you could have the best product or service in the world, but if the Relater doesn't like you, she will settle for second-best from a salesperson she feels more comfortable and secure with.

You can ask Relaters anything about the people side of the business. But, if possible, get the hard facts from someone else.

Be aware: If they don't like your product, Relaters are not likely to tell you so directly for fear of hurting feelings—both theirs and yours. So they may tell you instead what they think you are willing to hear.

The "Explore" Stage with Thinkers

Thinkers also make good interviewees because they like to answer questions that reveal their expertise. As long as you ask logical, fact-oriented questions that probe their knowledge, Thinkers are likely to talk to you.

Phrase your questions precisely and ask for precise answers. Thinkers relish detail and typically give short, crisp answers, even to open-ended questions. So, for the best dialogue, ask for the *exact* number of things, not the approximate number. For example, "How many copies per day must your copying machine produce?" or "Is that an average, or a maximum figure?"

Encourage Thinkers to ask you questions, too. If

they do and you don't have the answer, don't fake it. Promise to find the answer and get back to them in an agreed-upon time frame. And then do it.

3. The "Collaborate" Stage

The goal at the "Collaborate" stage is for you and your prospect to find a solution that meets the prospect's needs. You do this by taking the prospect's ideas and combining them with your own to arrive at a solution that makes sense to both of you.

Rather than using a monologue, the best salesperson engages in a *dialogue* to keep the prospect involved in a give-and-take. It's often a good idea to start by reviewing the points that were agreed upon in the last stage to make sure you and the prospect are still in agreement.

As you discuss a solution, explain how it will work in your customer's environment. Most customers don't care how something works; they want to know what it will do for them, how it will solve their problems. So the customer-smart salesperson speaks the language of *benefits* rather than *features*. A feature is some aspect of the whole product that exists regardless of a customer's needs. But a benefit is the way that feature satisfies a customer's need. A benefit, you might say, is a *feature in action*.

Our friend Carla, the computer salesperson, for instance, could say, "This computer has four megabytes of RAM" and hope the customer knows what that means for him. But a better way for Carla to put it might be: "This computer has four megabytes of RAM, which will allow you to run Windows, graphics applications, and other memory-intensive programs with greater speed, minimizing the waste of waiting time."

The "Collaborate" Stage with Directors

Gear your presentation toward the Director's priorities: saving time, getting results, being more efficient, achieving more success.

Due to lack of time, Directors don't evaluate ideas thoroughly. They prefer that you do the evaluating, then lay out options for their approval. Directors like quick, concise analyses of needs and solutions.

As you offer the analysis, skip over less important facts and cut to the bottom-line impact. You might say, "The way I see it, you can go with option A (tell its pros and cons), option B (tell its own pros and cons), or option C (tell its other pros and cons)."

Directors want to be in control. So give them choices backed with enough data to allow them to make intelligent decisions.

The "Collaborate" Stage with Socializers

Your presentation and your product should focus on how the Socializer's prestige, image, or recognition will grow. Talk about work relationships becoming more enjoyable and how the customer will look good with minimal added effort.

Your presentation should have impact, so involve as many of the senses as possible. So if you can show, for example, how sharp the product will look as well as how it will perform, so much the better.

The Socializer will want your presentation as well as the product to feel and look great. So your polish and grace will probably count for more with the Socializer than with the other styles.

Socializers also respond well to others' positive experiences. So, if you can, back up your claims with testimonials from well-known people or prestigious firms.

THE "COLLABORATE" STAGE WITH RELATERS

Show, if you can, how your product will stabilize, simplify, or support Relaters' way of doing things and their relationships. Present all changes in a non-threatening way.

You probably need to spend very little time explaining the features, unless the features make life easier. Involve the Relater in your presentation by having him or her give you feedback and answer questions.

Relaters like to know the appropriate steps to follow, so spell those out. Ask them to please share how they really feel about what you're recommending.

Make the point that the real benefit, in the final analysis, is that everything will run more smoothly.

THE "COLLABORATE" STAGE WITH THINKERS

Emphasize logic, accuracy, value, quality, and reliability. Show them how your product will assure that their company is on the right path in doing its job. Thinkers pride themselves on the accuracy of their analyses, so present your product in a way that shows they will be making the correct decision if they purchase your product.

Base that claim on facts, specifications, and other data. For example, point out cost-benefit analysis, maintenance costs, reliability figures, tax advantages, or statistics on increased efficiency. And when you talk about prices, relate them to specific benefits. Thinkers are very cost-conscious, so use hard facts to show that the expense will certainly be well worth it.

Thinkers are the most likely of the four behavioral styles to see the drawbacks. So you'll probably score points if you openly discuss your product's disadvantages. If you don't, Thinkers may see that omission as a coverup of this side in the "costs-benefits" (risks-rewards) analysis formula.

Make your points clearly. Then ask if further clarification is needed. It probably will be.

4. The "Commit" Stage

If you've done your job well in the first three stages—Contact, Explore, and Collaborate—the sale should close itself. It will flow naturally.

That's because top salespeople are always in step with their customers. They make sure there's agreement every step of the way. So by the time they get to the point of asking for the sale, it's a matter of *when*, not *if*.

But the ultimate goal is not just closing the sale and signing the paperwork. The ultimate goal is gaining a truly committed customer. So the "Commit" stage is critical in building a potential long-term partnership. It requires trust, respect, and open communication on each side. You can't work through all the stages of a sale and then at the end try a manipulative closing technique to clinch the deal. That doesn't make sense—and it doesn't work.

Both of you need the information the other has. If the customer has a concern, it's because he or she can see something you can't. So you need to find out what that is and address it.

Traditionally, salespeople are taught to overcome objections, as if the sales process were a contest. But savvy salespeople see objections differently. They view them not as rejections but as "midcourse corrections" that can steer you toward, not away from, your sales destination.

Think of "objections" as opportunities to make sure you have the right product matched to the customer's needs. If you don't, then pass up this sale and preserve the potential long-term relationship.

But if you've really done a good job of information-gathering since the beginning, if you've kept in step with your customer, and if you've confirmed agreement at each point, there should be few, if any, objections when you get to the "Commit" stage.

To best help your customers and clients, tailor the "Commit" stage to their personal styles.

THE "COMMIT" STAGE WITH DIRECTORS

You can come right out and ask them: Are you interested? Say something like, "Based on the points we've discussed, do you want to subscribe to our service?"

Usually they'll give you an answer in no uncertain terms. At times, though, Directors will appear to be unwise decision-makers. They can seem to procrastinate and put you off when, in fact, they aren't even thinking about you. They may be so busy and preoccupied that they literally haven't had time to evaluate your ideas. Or perhaps they think they don't have compelling information for taking action.

It's the salesperson's job, of course, to provide a convincing reason for the Director to close the deal. For example, when you call, you might say, "Some of the ways I thought we might be able to work together are X, Y, and Z. Could we discuss those when I call in a couple of weeks? Is there any more information I could get you in the meantime?"

If they do commit, write a short letter to them, explaining your commitment to seeing that results are achieved and pledging your help in attaining their goals.

The "Commit" Stage with Socializers

You can be open and just ask, "Where do we go from here?" or "What's the next step?"

Socializers are spontaneous. They respond well to the bandwagon approach of "Everyone's doing it" or "This offer is going to expire soon." In fact, they're so forward-moving and change-oriented that you may have to restrain them because they tend to overbuy, which can create buyer's remorse—and problems for you—later.

They're infamous for forgetting details. So make sure you put all the points in writing. If they protest that a written agreement isn't necessary, just say you need it to help *you* remember.

They don't like paperwork. So if any further forms or details are necessary, assure them that you'll take care of them yourself and that everything will be handled quickly and painlessly.

THE "COMMIT" STAGE WITH RELATERS

Relaters are much slower, more deductive decision-makers. Try not to rush them, but do provide gentle, helpful nudges.

Sometimes they are too reluctant to tell you in the Commit stage that they need more information because that's not what they think you want to hear. Be alert to that possibility and, if necessary, go back to the Collaborate stage and go over the information again.

Once the Relater is adequately informed, you should stress how the follow-through will be personalized for their particular situation. Show how the product or service will affect them and their co-workers positively.

You may need to lead them gently to commit by showing that you care. You might say something like, "Carl, we've talked about all the aspects of this, and I firmly believe this is the best solution for you. I wouldn't personally recommend it if I wasn't one hundred percent convinced that it'll work for you."

Relaters like guarantees. Assure them that the changes about to occur won't upset the applecart.

The "Commit" Stage with Thinkers

Thinkers are the most likely of all the styles to do comparison shopping. So mention your product's strengths and suggest that the Thinker compare those strengths to your competitor's.

Uncomfortable with snap decisions, Thinkers often need more information. So give them plenty of time to study the options. Also, be willing to reduce risk for Thinkers by giving them a trial run, a special guarantee, or other contingency "safety net" option.

But realize that sometimes they will say they need more time or information when, in fact, they actually are putting off making a decision. Your job is to provide them with the information until it reaches the point where the additional data isn't moving them closer to a decision.

At some point, you may need to be firm with Thinkers in a gentle way. You might say, "No problem, I can get that information for you. Will you then have enough background to make a decision?"

When you discuss the commitment letter, spell out exactly what the success criteria will be. Thinkers prefer specific means of measuring results.

5. The "Assure" Stage

This is where most salespeople drop the ball. They stop communicating after the customer has committed. The salesperson disappears, leaving installation, training, and follow-up service to someone else. But for the customer-smart salesperson, the real job starts when the customer says yes.

Assuring customer satisfaction is indispensable to exceptional sales success. If you make sure the customer is satisfied, you are more likely to get repeat business as well as referrals. Without those, you'll be continually cold-calling, not a likely path to success.

You can solidify your relationship with buyers by, first, being absolutely clear about their expectations. Ask them, "What are the criteria you'll use in judging the success of the purchase?" If you conducted the earlier stages well, you should already have a pretty good handle on those standards.

Monitor the criteria by staying involved with the customer or client. Write him or her a thank-you note. Give the customer a call to see if the product is performing as expected. Send him or her a token gift that will complement their purchase. And at least once a year, give the buyer an annual "checkup," a phone call, a drop-by, or a lunch at which you make sure they're happy and, if so, ask for referrals.

If there are problems with the product or service, see those not as setbacks but as a chance to show how much you care about your customers. Think long term. All future sales and referrals depend on your ability to reaffirm your commitment to quality and service.

As always, you can help by gearing your approach to the individual's personal style.

THE "ASSURE" STAGE WITH DIRECTORS

Remember, they're impatient. So if there's a problem and they don't hear from you, they'll jump ship and go to your competitor in nothing flat. So follow-up is crucial.

You know that their priority is control. So you should check with Directors to make sure they feel you've delivered on promised results. Your contact with them should be brief and to the point. Emphasize that you stand firmly behind your product, and assure them that follow-ups won't take up a lot of their time.

You might say, "You bought this to save time and effort. I want to make sure it continues to work for you. I'll periodically check back to make sure everything's running smoothly, but I won't waste your time with unnecessary calls. But if anything's less than what you expect, please call me and I'll fix it immediately."

Directors don't rely on personal relationships in business, so you can't assume that one sale means a lifetime of repeat business. Therefore, if problems do occur, be sure to respond immediately and with practical solutions.

THE "ASSURE" STAGE WITH SOCIALIZERS

Because they act so spontaneously, Socializers are more likely to regret a purchase than any of the other styles. They also may become quickly bored with the new purchase.

So you need to remind them that they made the right choice, that people feel good about their decision. You might also show them new uses for the product or new accessories that'll help keep the excitement alive. Give them plenty of service and assistance. Plus, be sure they're using the product correctly—Socializers who become frustrated due to incorrect usage often return the purchase for a refund.

Seek an up-tempo and highly personal relationship by contacting them regularly and meeting them face-to-face. An out-of-the-office chat, such as a casual breakfast, lunch, or after-work get-together, can be helpful. In any event, be prepared to spend some time. Socializers love visiting with people, especially in relaxed settings.

If any problems develop with your product or service, spare this customer any unnecessary time, effort, or complications. The payoff is that Socializers, if they're happy, will give you great word-of-mouth advertising. They mingle with a lot of people and are likely to talk up their satisfying purchases.

THE "ASSURE" STAGE WITH RELATERS

They'll need consistent, predictable, hands-on follow-through. Give them your personal assurance that you'll remain in touch, keep things running smoothly, and be available when needed.

Relaters will appreciate learning how to blend your new product or service with how they have always done things. You'll want to set up a simple, practical system for two-way communication that will let both of you monitor progress and deal with any glitches.

Because Relaters are actually change-resistant (especially when dealing with unfamiliar technology), you can help them by demonstrating how the product works, carefully leading them through a tryout experience, or arranging for the Relater to see the product successfully in use elsewhere. In all cases, focus on specific steps and shortcuts they can use.

Relaters see themselves as having built a friendship with you. So nurture that relationship with personal attention and offers of in-person visits and phone calls. And if a problem does occur, you should personally take care of it and explain to the Relater what happened and comfort him or her with how it will be avoided in the future.

The "Assure" Stage with Thinkers

Thinkers prefer to operate in a controlled, orderly, and error-free way. So, for starters, you should ask them how they'd prefer to organize your ongoing communications.

For example, how often would they like to meet? Where? And for how long? Keep in mind their stringent standards for products, services, and people. Make sure you're clear about their expectations of this new acquisition.

When you have your follow-up meetings, focus on *what* the product accomplished as well as *how well* it performed. Bring information on how this product has worked elsewhere. And ask them for data on your product or service's performance record.

If problems do occur, ask the Thinker directly, "If you were in my position, what would be a reasonable improvement action?" Then deliver on that solution and make sure you follow through until they're satisfied.

WORKING TOWARD A WIN-WIN

Treating your customers or clients the way *they* want to be treated, selling to them in the way *they* want to buy, is a strategy that can change your life. Thousands of salespeople have successfully applied **The Platinum Rule.** They've experienced dramatic increases in sales volumes as well as greater awareness of their own personal strengths and weaknesses.

You might want to follow the lead of one Illinois salesman. He reported a boost in sales when, after studying **The Platinum Rule,** he drafted four different follow-up letters, one to send to each of the four different personal styles he contacts.

Or you can even use your knowledge of behavioral styles as a guiding principle in how you organize your office. An insurance agent in charge of a small New England operation began using **The Platinum Rule** concept to recruit other agents, to show them how to maximize their strengths, and to teach them how to sell better. Within three years, his office became the largest in his company and the biggest insurance agency in the region.

A FUNDAMENTAL CHANGE

What we've described may be a fundamental change in the way you've been selling. If you begin following **The Platinum Rule,** you may, in effect, be changing jobs. You may be changing from a person who "sells" things, who sees a sale as a one-shot event, who sees your customers merely as people who can help your career, to a person who "consults" and "solves problems" based on your knowledge of your customers' personal needs and desires.

As you work at developing a win-win solution with everyone, you'll find there's a side benefit. Not only will your business improve, but you'll also find you'll make many new friends along the way. You'll be building lifetime loyalty to your product or service—and to yourself as well.

11

♦

PROVIDING SERVICE
WITH STYLE

Eric, a bank loan officer, called it "the workday from
hell." There'd been a mix-up so terrible that his tem-
ples ached and his stomach churned.

Somehow, a number of applications for mortgage
refinancing loans had gotten scrambled. As a result,
some well-qualified applicants were wrongly turned
down because of "bad credit." But while their credit
isn't really bad, Eric learned, some of their tempers
are.

Eric's phone has been ringing all morning. Several
other angry customers even came to the bank to confront him. Now he's dreading picking up the phone
and he's almost afraid to look up from his desk. That's
because the problem is even more widespread than
Eric first believed. How can he deal with these people
in a way that will preserve the bank's reputation,
soothe the customers' wounded pride, and keep his
job secure?

Eric, while not yet sure of the answer, remembers

something curious about the complaints. While all the customers suffered the same fate—being falsely labeled as credit risks—their reactions ran the gamut from furious to resigned.

"I won't ever deal with your bank again even if you paid me," one declared. "And neither will any of my family or friends. I'd live in a tent, in a cardboard box even, before I'd do business with you people. And, believe me, buddy, everybody I know will hear about this."

But others, though distressed, were calm and low-key. One, in fact, was almost apologetic. "Gee, I guess I can see how this could happen," she said. "But I'm sure you can understand how upsetting it is. What's done is done, though. What can I do now to get this loan back on track other than going elsewhere?"

Eric yearned for a way out of this mess. He needed a way to handle each of these people so that they'd be satisfied, the bank would emerge relatively unscathed, and his blood pressure would return to something approximating normal.

What Eric needed to know was how to create . . .

"A Moment of Magic!"

THE IMPORTANCE OF SERVICE

Everywhere you turn today, you hear about the importance of service, support, and customer satisfaction. All kinds of firms proclaim that the customer is king, that "people are our business," that satisfaction is the company's highest goal.

With all this talk, you'd think that service would be getting better all the time. Surveys, though, suggest otherwise.

Consider:

- One customer in four is said to be thinking about leaving the average business at any given time because of dissatisfaction.
- For every complaint actually received the average business has 26 customer problems, 6 of which are "serious."

What's wrong? With so much talk about service, why aren't customers being treated the way they want to be treated?

One reason is that too many companies and employees view customer support as an occurrence, something that happens once and then is over. But excellent service really focuses not on a one-time event but on building a sustained, positive relationship.

Those who see service that way understand that any business consists of a series of customer encounters. Success comes from managing those encounters in a way that builds long-term relationships. To do so requires treating people well, including employees, because how employees are treated by upper management sets the tone for how those employees, in turn, deal with the customers. Treating people well— whether customer or workers—involves showing courtesy, recognition, caring, and sincerity. It entails working hard to build rapport and trust by communicating well and often. It means being sensitive to individual differences.

Firms and people with a positive attitude toward service know that just doing their job is not enough. They know that each contact—even a conflict or a complaint—is an opportunity that may never come again. That opportunity can be used to build, or rebuild, a successful relationship. Or to destroy it.

If you use **The Platinum Rule** to guide your service, you'll know how customers want to be treated. And by treating them that way, you can help ensure success for yourself and your firm.

PUT YOURSELF IN THE CUSTOMER'S SHOES

Think of your own experience with service. Each encounter at the dry cleaners, the grocery, the auto-repair shop contributes to your decision of whether you're going to continue to do business there. Each dealing adds to, or subtracts from, your satisfaction.

Such service encounters typically fall into three categories:

Moments of Magic: Positive experiences that make customers glad they do business there.
Moments of Misery: Negative experiences that irritate, frustrate, or annoy.
Moments of Mediocrity: Routine, uninspired service that leaves neither a strong positive impression nor a strong negative impression.

Moments of Magic might include a hotel clerk who welcomes you with a warm smile, uses your name, shakes your hand, and sincerely asks that you call her if you run into any problems. Or the man at the dry cleaners who offers to pick up your clothing at your office if that would save you a trip. Or offers to re-clean for free a suit that didn't come out just right.

Or the phone-company representative whom you ask to switch your phone to a new home: She thanks you for holding, efficiently but courteously takes your information, comments on where you're moving, and urges you, if you have other questions or problems, to call her on her direct line.

You remember such experiences. But you probably remember even more clearly the Moments of Misery, such as clerks who won't take responsibility for solving a problem. Personnel who don't know what they're doing—and worse yet, don't seem to care. Employees who are rude or inattentive. Salespeople who, after ignoring you, finally acknowledge your presence but then act as if they're doing you a favor by taking your money.

We've all had those experiences, too. But usually not more than once at the same place. Because we don't go back!

THE BASIC EXPECTATIONS

The key to creating a Moment of Magic is exceeding a customer's expectations. Sounds simple enough. But actually customers evaluate service on two levels:

Performance and Personal, according to our associates Gregg Baron and Robert Coates of Success Sciences, Inc. in Tampa, Florida.

At the *Performance level*, customers judge you on the quality and efficiency of the tasks you perform. Did you provide accurate information? Did you follow up as promised? Do you have the needed expertise?

The *Personal level*, on the other hand, is about how the customer feels he or she was treated. Did you make the customer feel valued? Were you courteous? Did you really listen?

Both levels affect customer satisfaction. You can get what you request (Performance level) but if it's delivered in a rude, curt manner (Personal level), it can still create a Moment of Misery.

Customers' expectations can vary from one business to another and from situation to situation. But here are some basic expectations that customers have of personnel in a service encounter:

Interest	Customers want someone who cares about them and their needs.
Flexibility	Each customer believes his or her situation is unique. Customers want you to respond to that unique need.
Problem-solving	When there's a problem, the customer wants the first person they talk with to assume responsibility: Either take care of the problem, or get all the information needed to enable the customer to take care of it.

Recovery   When a customer's expectations aren't met, that customer wants some word or gesture that shows you're concerned and want to make it up to him. Recovery can be used to turn a Moment of Misery into a Moment of Magic.

CUSTOMERS ARE DIFFERENT

As Eric, the beleaguered bank loan officer, discovered, complaining customers can be a diverse bunch: some loudly belligerent, some upset but overloading him with details, others low-key and almost apologetic.

But it's not just the customers who vary. *We*, the service providers, also have different ways of reacting. Some people in business find the apologetic customer irritating and the belligerent customer perfectly understandable. Others find the belligerent one rude and intimidating and the apologetic one polite. And yet others are put off by the customer who recounts every detail of the problem instead of concentrating on a solution.

So, to give successful service, we must approach people flexibly. If Eric responds the same way to the apologetic, the demanding, and the detail-oriented customer, he might increase the tension for at least two of them. He might even produce a Moment of Misery.

DIFFERENT SETS OF LENSES

Our beliefs, expectations, knowledge, and needs create a unique filter for each of us. We don't look at people and situations through the same set of lenses. To a Relater, the Director may seem pushy, overbearing, and difficult, while to another Director, he or she might be seen as strong, capable, and motivated. That person's behavior wouldn't have changed, but the reaction to that behavior could vary widely.

Besides, in a service situation, the employee has information and feelings the customer is unaware of. For instance, a sense of how hard this firm really tries to be fair, how truly caring management may be, how few mistakes may really occur compared to the total number of transactions.

And the customers have information and feelings that employees don't, for example, why they really were counting on having this loan quickly approved. Or maybe customers bring other bad experiences they've had with financial institutions to the situation.

The more you understand your customers' views, the better you can help them understand yours. Knowing the behavioral styles of your customers will help you see their view, as will other skills we'll talk about in this chapter.

Some people resist the idea of adapting their communication style to build rapport with others. "I'm *me*—and they can take me or leave me," they say, in effect. But if you want to get your message across—and that's a major part of what any business is about—you'll be more successful if you present your message in a way that's easy for others to understand. By being flexible and reducing tension, you increase the chances that you'll be heard and, as a consequence, that you and your business will be successful.

CUSTOMERS UNDER STRESS

Let's get back to our beleaguered friend Eric. How can he best handle the complaints about the botched loan applications? How should he deal with complaints from each of the four behavioral styles?

First, Eric needs to know something about how each style usually responds to *stress*. Customers with a complaint often feel a great deal of pressure; they spent money for something they "thought" they needed. Now the money's gone, and the product or service isn't working out as they expected.

But all of their stress may not originate with you or even with your product or service. The customer may have had a fight with his or her spouse, been reprimanded at work, and *then*, in this case, discovered the glitch in the loan process. While Eric and the bank are not the sole sources of the stress, they are available targets.

Each behavioral style shows different symptoms of stress and reacts in different ways. Each style has its own characteristic—but usually unproductive—way of venting. If Eric recognizes these patterns and understands that the customer is venting on him because he's an available target, that in itself can reduce the stress.

He can just recognize that this is, say, a Director, who's feeling a lot of pressure, and being a very direct person, is responding accordingly. That's more productive than Eric thinking, What a jerk! Why's he yelling at me? or, even worse, yelling back.

What the customers need from Eric to help them reduce their stress will vary according to style. If Eric can deal with each customer in a way that addresses his or her needs under stress, he'll reduce the tension on both sides.

Directors

As complainants, they can be highly critical and blunt. Often aggressive and sometimes pushy, they can become intrusive, perhaps saying something like "I demand to see the bank president this instant!" or "If you don't furnish me a copy of every last bit of correspondence in this case, you'll hear from my lawyer."

Directors may appear uncooperative, and they'll often act as if they want to control everything. "I'm not filling out one more piece of paper," they might say in response to your request that they file an official complaint. "It's your turn to push the pencil, buddy."

When their backs are to the wall, Directors can become dictators. At least that's how they often appear. But what do they *need?* What can Eric do to settle them down and get this all resolved?

Directors will want to see:

- tangible evidence of progress;
- a fast pace;

- that they have control of the situation;
- results; and
- that time is being saved.

So Eric, in dealing with frustrated loan applicants who are Directors, would do well to show them what's already been done. Perhaps a letter of apology is being prepared, or there's an internal memo ordering the loan applications of these wronged customers to be expedited.

The last thing Eric should do is try to assert his authority and argue with the Directors. They're not going to be listening, and they'll probably outassert him.

"Nobody ever won an argument with a customer" is an axiom of service. And that's doubly true with Directors.

Socializers

When they have a service problem, Socializers may seem overeager and impulsive. "I need this settled right this moment," they may say, despite your logical explanation of why this complex situation can't possibly be cleared up for forty-eight hours.

It may be difficult to pin down what exactly would settle the issue for them. One minute they may sound reasonable; the next moment they're being sarcastic and making unrealistic, and even frenzied, demands.

Socializers, who are usually skilled in verbal attack, may also come across as manipulative. They might say, "I wonder if a letter to the chairman of your parent firm as well as to the state Board of Bank Examiners would improve your response time?"

Under stress, Socializers' primary response may be to disregard the facts and anything you say. That's the way they appear. But how could banker Eric best deal with Socializers who feel wronged? What *needs* do they have that he can meet?

Socializers will respond best to:

- personal attention;
- a quick pace;
- affirmation of their position;
- lots of verbal give-and-take; and
- seeing that effort is being saved.

Eric may think the best course is to sit there impassively and let the Socializers harangue him. But, actually, he'll be better off to engage actively with them and involve them, giving a quick-paced, spirited explanation that shows he isn't just brushing them off. Socializers need to know he truly cares and is paying attention, that he appreciates the uniqueness of their case, and that he finds them engaging even when they're upset.

Relaters

Relaters are the least likely to be loud and argumentative. When they do come forward, Relaters may appear submissive, hesitant, wishy-washy, or even apologetic.

Worse yet, they may not even complain openly but just internalize their dissatisfaction and take their business elsewhere. So if you suspect a problem, you may even need to draw them out.

Relaters hate conflict, so they just wish this whole flap over the loan applications would go away, even if it's not necessarily settled in their favor. "I'm sorry to make such a big deal out of this," they might say, "but my credit's really quite good, and being turned down for that reason doesn't really make much sense as far as I can see. What can be done about this?"

Or they may sometimes get a little defensive. "Well, I've never had this kind of problem before, you know, and I don't enjoy being portrayed as some kind of deadbeat." But usually their basic response to high stress is not to make waves, to submit.

How can Eric tailor his response to put Relaters most at ease?

Relaters will be made most comfortable by:

- assuring them they're personally okay;
- promising that the crisis will soon ebb;
- showing that the loan reapplication process will be relaxed and pleasant;
- suggesting that he's committed to working with them to iron out the problem; and
- indicating that the "relationship" is being saved.

After all the flak he's endured, Eric may be tempted to see the quiet Relater complainant as somebody he can brush aside with mere lip service, someone who doesn't have to be taken very seriously. But Eric must remind himself that the Relaters are just as upset as the Directors; they just express it in a much more subtle way.

So Relaters don't like to complain and don't do so

very forcefully. But, again, remember: They're not captive customers, and they'll go elsewhere if their needs aren't met. If Eric wants to keep their business, he'll do well to assure them in a friendly, personal way that this loan foul-up is just a fleeting blip on life's radar screen—not a fundamental change in the business routine.

Thinkers

Complaints from Thinkers will also visually be less direct, like those from Relaters—but with a sharper edge to them. They won't loudly carp and cajole like Directors or Socializers, but they won't be submissive, either.

Thinkers tend to recite the chronology of events and the litany of errors they've had to endure. They may explain the painstaking care with which they filled out the loan application. They may act a bit hurt that, despite all their effort and conscientious adherence to the rules, their loan was turned down for illogical reasons.

Thinkers won't be the quickest to complain. But when they do, they'll likely provide data and documentation and get quite involved in the sequence and details of the snafu.

"I don't understand how this could happen," they might say. "My credit record is spotless—I take some pride in that—and I gave you all the information you asked for. I spent days filling out those forms, trying to be as accurate as possible. I even included a cover letter in which I asked you to call me if any hitches developed. The next thing I know, I've been rejected for credit reasons. This defies both sound business practices and common sense."

Faced with an unyielding foe, Thinkers will likely withdraw. They may cut the conversation short and leave—and take their bank business with them, never to return.

How can a person like Eric lessen tension with complaining Thinkers?

Here's how:

- Suggest that they're right.
- Explain the process and the details.
- Indicate appreciation of their accuracy and thoroughness.
- Deal with them in a way that permits thorough processing of their key concerns and questions.
- Help them "save face."

Eric may see the Thinkers as compulsives more hung up on the process and on showing that they're right than concerned about getting the loan applications back on track. But if he wants to retain their loyalty, he'll end this episode on a positive note by being flexible. He'll deal with them precisely and systematically, emphasizing the bank's interest in seeing justice done—and done in an accurate, structured, rational way.

CUSTOMER-DRIVEN VERSUS OPERATIONS-DRIVEN

If Eric uses **The Platinum Rule,** he'll see these wronged customers through the prism of their personal styles. Then he can adapt to their needs. Doing so will go a long way toward making himself and his bank *customer-driven*, a key to good service.

Consider your own buying habits. What most attracts you as a consumer? The lowest price? Sometimes, but probably not always. More likely, it's getting the most *value*. When you find that, you return again and again. Businesses can provide a greater value than their competitors by being customer-driven—making the customer feel like he or she counts for something more than just a sale.

Businesses project either a customer-driven or an operations-driven mentality. They either try to serve primarily the customer, or they seek to serve mainly the business itself. As employees, we have a choice between doing what's best for us or what's best for the client.

The operations-driven firm looks for ways to make things best for its owners or employees. It creates systems, procedures, and controls to protect itself. Maybe it opens late and/or closes early. Or makes a customer fill out a long form before he or she can get a refund. Or doesn't make the effort to post its prices clearly.

Customers get the impression that they're not very important, or maybe are even a bit of a burden. The attitude of operations-driven businesses is "How can we sell something?" Its salespeople emphasize the product and its features. Its employees seem to be thinking, If it weren't for all these customers, we could get our job done!

VALUING THE CUSTOMER

By contrast, the customer-driven business creates policies and procedures that are helpful and friendly to its customers. Like a bank that's open on Saturdays. Or a department store that has a generous merchandise-return policy. Or an auto dealership that calls to see how your new car is performing.

Rather than being made to feel burdensome, the customer feels important. The customer-driven business asks "How can we help people?" and "How can we make it easy and gratifying for people to do business with us?" Its salespeople stress the customer's needs more than the product's features. Its employees' philosophy: "If it weren't for our customers, we wouldn't have a job!"

Operations-driven companies may see customers as an interruption of work. But the customer-driven firm sees them as the purpose of it. While the operations-driven firm has its eye solely on the bottom line, the customer-driven company focuses on its clients or customers. When there's an economic downturn, the operations-driven business just looks for ways to cut costs. The customer-driven firm seeks ways to lure more customers, thus improving its sales and profitability.

Years ago, companies often distinguished themselves from their competitors by their products. Cars didn't mostly look alike, beers by and large didn't taste the same, soaps didn't all clean basically the same way. But now, technology for making cars, beer, soap—and most everything else—is duplicated so quickly that many products are very similar, regardless of brand.

So one of the ways a business can set itself apart is by being customer-driven. And knowing and using **The Platinum Rule** is a way for employees to be much more attentive to the wants and needs of their customers and clients.

PRINCIPLES OF CUSTOMER-DRIVEN SERVICE

Let's examine some of the key principles that define customer-driven service and see how **The Platinum Rule** can help.

■ *People do not buy things, they buy expectations.* It helps to get as much information as possible about the expectations of your customers or clients. You can use **The Platinum Rule** to quickly establish rapport that will draw your customers out. Many businesses fail because they believe customers buy "things," such as computer software. But a customer buying software is really buying a solution to certain problems.

If you or your salespeople deal with customers simply on a level of "things," the customer's decision will be based largely on price. But if they see your product or service as a value-added purchase, they'll be willing to pay more for it because it's not just a commodity they're buying. They're also buying your knowledge and interest in them and their problem.

Using **The Platinum Rule,** you can quickly build a bond with customers, learn their expectations, and meet those expectations.

■ *Close contact with customers must be maintained.* Before you design a new product or service, go out into the marketplace and, using **The Platinum Rule** principles, talk with your customers or potential customers. Try to get them to tell you the intimate details about what's really important to them, why they do business with you, what they like and don't like.

Knowing the personal styles and being able to adapt to them will give you an edge in discovering this data.

■ *When two people really want to do business together, they won't let details stand in the way.* People want to do business with people they like and trust. If you practice rapport with your clients using **The Platinum Rule,** they'll like and trust you more.

Then, when a problem occurs, the customer's attitude is going to be, "How are *we* going to handle this?" Lacking that strong relationship, they're more likely to think and say, *"You've* got a problem. What are *you* going to do about it?"

(Incidentally, the words *customer* and *client* as used throughout this chapter and the previous one, create an image of a buyer of services or products. But it's important to note that a "customer" isn't always on the "outside." Many of those references can and should apply as well to internal "customers," such as, say, the operating divisions served by the personnel department. You can use **The Platinum Rule** to build important bridges to clients within the organization, too.)

YOUR CHALLENGE

If you want exceptionally satisfied customers who, in turn, will create positive word-of-mouth advertising for you, you need to create many Moments of Magic, not Moments of Misery or Moments of Mediocrity.

To do that you must exceed their expectations. Knowing and using **The Platinum Rule** gives you an important head start. Because if you can read people's behavioral styles, you'll have a pretty good idea of how they expect to be treated. Treat them that way and you can create a strong personal relationship that practically guarantees a Moment of Magic every time that customer walks into your store or office.

On the other hand, if you don't know or care about a customer's expectations, you run a very strong chance of sowing dissatisfaction, of creating a Moment of Misery. A friend of ours, for instance, went into a mall store specializing in athletic shoes. The walls were lined with a bewildering array of shoes of all types and styles: running shoes, cross-trainers, basketball shoes, walking shoes, court shoes, hiking shoes. Our friend, being a Thinker, had, of course, given much thought to his needs, and he arrived at the store with a mental list of desired features.

When a clerk came bounding up to ask if he could help, the Thinker began, "I run four to five miles two to three times a week. On grass, usually. But I also play basketball outdoors on hardtop once every couple of weeks and would like a shoe that's good for that, too.

"Plus, I have very flat feet. So it's important that my shoes have exceptionally good arch support. Which of these models," he concluded, pointing to the scores of shoes on display, "do you think would most closely meet those criteria?"

Clearly, this was a customer who had an expectation of being given detail. He wasn't going to buy a shoe just because it was stylish or cheap or because the clerk was charismatic.

But none of that registered with this clerk. He smiled broadly, probably in a way he thought was irresistibly charming, and replied offhandedly, "Well, you know what people say: 'Shoes are shoes.' They're all pretty much the same."

The Thinker was stunned. He'd described his problem earnestly and thoroughly and had been told, in effect, that it really wasn't a problem. After muttering to himself, "Well, money is money, and I'll take mine elsewhere," the Thinker spun on his heels and left the store, never to return. The clerk, clearly a stranger to **The Platinum Rule** and customer-driven service, had created a customer *for a competitor!*

The clerk had taken the easy way out, opting not to explain the differences among the shoes or to find another clerk who could explain. The clerk chose not to adapt but to use the same approach with this customer as he likely did with every other. It might have worked with a Socializer. Or maybe even with a Relater. But definitely not with a Thinker or a Director.

DEFUSING CONFLICT

Sometimes, though, even if you try to be customer-driven, there will be a conflict. Problems happen.

No matter how good you are, how committed you are, how much effort you make to give superior service, eventually something will go wrong. It may not even have anything to do with you. But still, it can occur, and what you have on your hands is a genuine Moment of Misery.

A customer experiencing a Moment of Misery typically feels one of three degrees of dissatisfaction:

BOTHERED   Customers are bothered when service falls short of expectations. This disappoints or negatively surprises the customers, but it doesn't inconvenience them.

IRRITATED   Customers become irritated when annoyed by poor service, are somewhat inconvenienced, or have lost time but *not* money.

ABUSED   Customers feel abused when they're grossly inconvenienced, have lost time *and* money, and feel personally insulted or unfairly treated, or made angry or upset.

When handling complaining customers, it's important to determine to what degree they're dissatisfied. The more upset they are, the greater and faster your efforts must be to correct the situation and turn it into a Moment of Magic. That's called conflict resolution, or recovery.

Here are some ways to foster recovery, as suggested by our associates Gregg Baron and Robert Coates:

1. Listen.

A lot of sales and service problems can be reduced, or even eliminated, by listening well. That's one of the keys to reading the personal styles, as we've seen, and one of the keys to creating Moments of Magic.

Most customers, finding themselves in a conflict, feel a need to get their point across. So they talk, often a lot and loudly. Your first impulse also may be to explain or defend.

If you want to defuse the emotion, though, talking first is not the way to do it. While you are talking, the customer or client is usually not listening but, instead, is merely awaiting his or her turn to sound off.

It's usually better to let the customer vent. Getting rid of that anger is often a first step toward a solution. For one thing, it reduces the pent-up pressure. After expressing his irritation, the customer then is usually ready to go on to the next step. Secondly, he or she may be pleasantly surprised that you listened to the complaint without fighting back. The customer can see that you're less interested in arguing with him than in fixing the problem.

In fact, the greatest power and control in any conflict rests with the one who actually *hears* what the other person is saying. So the first step in easing tension is to truly listen.

Eric, for example, if he is listening closely, may

hear one of his miffed bank customers suggest that, though they're displeased at having their credit questioned, they're much more unhappy about the delay in getting their loan. If that's the case, Eric should spend less time explaining the mix-up and more time expediting the loan process. That way he'd most please the customer and also ease his own distress.

So listen to your customers' complaints but also listen for clues about their behavioral styles. Are they fast-paced, or slower-paced? Task-oriented or relationship-oriented? Inclined to think in terms of facts, or in terms of feelings? Remind yourself what those clues tell you about how this conflict might best be resolved.

2. Apologize.

This is a crucial gesture that's often forgotten in the heat of battle. Eric, for example, should offer a sincere, personal apology—from *him*, not the bank—that shows he's committed to the relationship.

3. Ask questions.

Gather as much information as possible. Ask the customers to give you their view of events. Not just the facts, but also their *feelings* about the facts.

How questions are asked is another telltale difference between operations-driven and customer-driven businesses. Operations-driven firms tend to ask few questions and follow their own agenda for fixing the problem. Customer-driven organizations, on the other hand, query the customer in depth. That way they are likely to solve the problem quickly as well as learn enough to keep it from happening again. The customer-driven firm also tries to follow the customer's timetable for getting the situation resolved.

Careful questioning, though it may take a few minutes longer initially, often reduces the overall time needed to handle a problem. Ask questions that will get you the information you need to help the customer. That way you'll stay in control while moving the transaction along quickly, yet professionally.

Eric, for instance, should find out when the loan seekers first applied, how much time has been lost, what kind of a deadline they're operating under, and what kind of costs they might have incurred as a result of the delay. If he does that, he'll soon know how much damage has been done and how he can best repair it.

4. Align with the customer.

As strange as it may seem, upset customers generally want to be *understood* even more than they want to have their problem solved. So respond in a way that shows you understand their position. Be sure you make them feel heard, especially if they seem emotionally involved in the situation.

Take care of the Personal level issues first. Usually if you attempt to deal with customers on a Performance level before acknowledging them on a Personal level, they become even more upset.

So, if possible, find some common thread on which to focus the discussion. Often this may be simply

275

agreeing on what the problem is. Eric might tell his customers, "I can see why you might feel that way. Most people, myself included, take pride in their credit standing." Or "Such a situation would be upsetting to me, too." Even if he can't really identify with their anger, Eric could empathize by saying something like "I see what you mean. Your viewpoint is clear and understandable."

5. Examine options.

Working with available options, try to create a win-win situation. Ask the customer what might work for him or her, then figure out if the two of you can make it happen.

Ask questions that will get the customer involved in the process, such as "How would you like to see this problem resolved?" or "What would be an acceptable resolution for you?" or "If you were in my position, how might you resolve this for *your* customer?"

In Eric's case, for instance, the disappointed loan applicants will likely feel better if he tells them the alternatives and perhaps the timetable and pros and cons of each option. That's preferable to Eric merely saying, "We made a mistake, we're sorry, and here's what *you* need to do."

6. Jump through hoops.

Make the recovery process easy for your customer. If, for instance, there are phone calls to make to the credit agency or bank forms to fill out, Eric can help them with it. If resolving the problem is going to be complicated, Eric should explain the procedure to the customer. People feel better when they at least know what's involved and how long it's going to take.

7. Offer "compensation"—a "goodwill" (faith) token.

If the Moment of Misery was extreme enough—as it probably was in Eric's case—the employee should say "I'm sorry" with a tangible gesture of some kind. While it doesn't need to be expensive, the gift should be:

- *Immediate*: Giving a gift long after the fact makes it seem meaningless and insincere.
- *Valuable*: The gift should have meaningful perceived value for the customer and should also differentiate the bank from its competitors. (Be creative! Don't send flowers or candy—everyone does that. Know your customer well enough that you'll know whether a pair of tickets to the ball game or a hot-air balloon ride would be more appropriate.)
- *Consumable*: Customers should be able to consume the gift relatively soon. Otherwise, if it's, say, a calendar or a clock, it might actually remind them of your mistake every time they look at it. The best gift to mend a Moment of Misery is one that's appreciated, then goes out of sight and out of mind.

8. Follow up.

After resolving the problem, with or without a gift, you must follow up. This is essential because there's nothing worse than the solution itself getting fouled up; that's the way to lose a customer forever.

Eric should contact all the aggrieved customers to make sure that they got the right paperwork, if any, and that they understand it and the reason for it. He should call again when their loans are funded to make sure all went well.

STAYING PROFESSIONAL IF ATTACKED

Those suggestions should serve you well with most customers. But some complainants are more than just angry and emotional. They actually get verbally abusive. They might make insulting remarks or take "cheap shots" as you try to help them. When that happens, it's very important to remain calm and professional.

For most of us, the knee-jerk response to a very angry, critical customer is either to get equally upset or to surrender. But neither is very productive. A better option is to try to remain composed and not take the attacks personally.

Remember, handle *the person first, then the problem.* Give them some time to vent their frustration. As we mentioned earlier, this alone may go a long way toward resolving the conflict.

Listen very closely and objectively to what the customer is saying. Try to find something you can align with. Maybe it's just a reassuring "You have a point there" or "I absolutely can see what you mean" or "I definitely understand." The idea is to meet the customer with no resistance. When the customer doesn't get the expected resistance, that can largely remove you as a target and allow both you and the customer to move ahead toward solving the problem.

A LASTING ANNUITY

The moral of the story: If you go out of your way to provide good service, if you make an effort to understand your customer's personal style and adapt to it, if you practice empathy and good communication, if you collaborate with your customer in solving the problem, your customers aren't likely to make outrageous demands, become abusive, or take their business elsewhere.

All they really want, after all, is a good return on their expenditure. If they get that and you give them a Moment of Magic, they'll pay you back with more purchases and referrals.

A customer who's treated well is a true annuity. Studies show that customers who feel that a business responds to their complaints are more likely than noncomplainers to do business there again. They actually become *more loyal than if the problem never happened.*

So look at your customer-service problems as opportunities. See them as chances to show how much you really care about the customer.

In handling service problems, you first need to acknowledge the difficulty immediately and take responsibility for your part in it. Then do whatever is needed to resolve the problem. This could range, for instance, from writing a letter of apology to refunding all or part of the cost. Confirm with the customer that your solution is a satisfactory one for him or her. And whatever you're going to do, do it quickly.

Too many firms say, "No, no, no," and then, after they've squandered all customer goodwill, they say yes. Saying yes upfront will go a long way toward building customer loyalty. And customer loyalty is money in the bank. It generally can cost from five to seven times more to get a new customer than to retain an old one.

Many of us were taught that a company's function is to make money. But, actually, that's a measure of achieving its function. Its *function* is to get and keep customers. So as service problems occur, bear in mind that there's more at issue than just the profit from this one sale. At stake are all future sales and referrals from this customer.

Eric's "workday from hell" wasn't fun, but it was instructive. He spoke with each bank customer affected by the loan mix-up. He apologized, and then listened to them until his ears practically ached. But he made note of their personal differences and then adapted his own style, being careful to handle the matter, first, at the Personal level, then at the Performance level.

For the Directors, Eric succinctly pledged a turnaround that would get them results—soon. With Socializers, he was more chatty and expressive and was quick to relieve them of almost all follow-up paperwork. Relaters he treated with special gentleness, assuring them that he was committed to working with them to restore their successful relationship with the bank. And to Thinkers he delivered a thorough explanation of what had gone wrong and how that was definitely going to change.

To all, he gave a convincing handshake, made eye contact, mentioned the customer's name, was quick to say "please" and "thank you," and ended the encounter with some type of friendly closing. A few days later all the aggrieved customers got a small, thoughtful gift in the mail as well as a call from Eric asking if the loan reapplication was working out all right.

ERIC'S LAW

Even the most vociferous of the complainants had calmed down by then and seemed genuinely pleased to hear from Eric. One man, whom Eric had pegged as a Director, said he was going to mention Eric's efficiency to the bank president at the next Kiwanis Club meeting. And one woman, identified by Eric as a Relater, actually said she was so impressed by his handling of the dispute that she planned to open another account with the bank.

This wasn't lost on Eric's boss. He congratulated Eric on making good on the bank's advertising slogan

("Our Biggest Asset Is a Satisfied Customer") and assured him that the firm's higher-ups would soon hear of Eric's triumph at damage control.

Eric hoped that meant he was about to be "discovered" by the top brass and soon would be on the fast track upward. But, in any event, he knew he'd made a lasting discovery of his own, one that would serve him well at this firm or any other.

He called it "Eric's Law": *Your customers aren't just part of your job, your customers are your career!*

12

♦

CHANGING THE REST OF YOUR LIFE BY CREATING POSITIVE RELATIONSHIPS

We know a guy who practiced **The Platinum Rule**—and got a house as a result! An unwitting participant in a real-estate bidding war, he got the home even though his bid was only the second highest. Surprised, he asked why. The seller said merely, "I *liked* you better."

That's a simple, powerful example of the power of **The Platinum Rule.** By choosing how we act, we can encourage others to respond more positively. This works not only for adults in the workplace but for people of all ages in all of life's other arenas: home, school, sports, shopping, you name it! Anywhere you seek better relationships, you can, with practice, transform your experiences into positive results.

Being the best person you can be by treating people the way *they* want to be treated pays off enormously. And not just in making a sale or negotiating a deal. Rather, the big dividend comes in creating a web of rich relationships that makes for a fuller life.

A recent study in the *Journal of the American Medical Association*, for example, reported that physicians who had never been sued were most likely to be seen by their patients as concerned, accessible, and willing to answer questions. Conversely, doctors were more likely to be sued if their patients feel they were arrogant, rude, and rushing the visits. The latter group of doctors, in other words, are showing less flexibility, and in this case they're paying for it.

The value of adaptability can't be overstated. It's a linchpin of **The Platinum Rule** and the key to building successful relationships of all kinds. Flexible people realize that there is a difference between their self (who they are) and their behavior (how they choose to act). Flexible people consciously decide whether and how to respond to a person, a situation, or an event.

Less adaptable people, on the other hand, respond in a more habitual manner, regardless of whether the response is likely to be appropriate or effective. They're sort of like mules, plodding along by putting down one foot after another without much thought. Mules are good for some things, of course, but they're not known for adapting their behavior to fit the circumstances. That's why they've come to symbolize stubborn resistance.

But even if you're a "mule," even if you are a person who's been wedded to your own ways of thinking and doing for a very long time, there is hope. You can commit to learning to be more flexible. Reducing your rigid behavior will make you more successful in your dealings with everyone, from the trashman to the movie usher to the company president.

Besides, by now, you're already more than halfway

there! You know your own behavioral style, or combination of styles. You know the other styles and how to identify them. You've got a pretty good idea about what you need to do to adapt to others.

But you still may find all this difficult to actually *do*. You can't expect to change a lifetime's habitual patterns overnight. But you can *begin to change*—if you are really committed.

Here are some pointers on how to become more adaptable, how to nudge yourself toward transcending the confines of your own style:

1. *Welcome, don't shun, different types of situations or activities.* Introduce some novelty into your life by not always doing things the same old way. Maybe, for example, you should try wearing a bolo tie. They look dorky, you say? You may be right. But experience what a bolo tie looks like and feels like on you. At worst, it'll become a conversational icebreaker with your friends, who'll wonder what's come over you!

Are you a regular salad-for-lunch person? Then tomorrow eat a submarine sandwich, with meat, cheese and lots of mayo. Once won't kill you. Millions of people enjoy them daily, and maybe you'll understand why.

Watch a TV show you'd normally avoid. Go to an art exhibit featuring a genre you're not fond of. And if you normally hold back at parties, try boldly going around the room and introducing yourself and see what happens.

None of these small rebellions is going to change your life. But becoming more aware of other people's feelings and actions, their likes and dislikes—in short,

their *differences*—is a key to developing more mutually satisfying relationships.

And this is especially true if you're a rigid person. If
you prefer to lock quickly onto one meaning, one
outcome, or one way of acting or thinking, then
these tiny challenges to habit may help you take off
the blinders. You may start to see that there needn't
be walls built between the way you do and see things
and how others do and see them.

2. *Don't jump to conclusions about people.* Let's say a
fast-talking salesperson in a plaid blazer and white
duck trousers appears at your door. Before deciding
that he's obviously a sharpie out to fleece you, at
least take the time to listen to his pitch. Maybe he
won't end up as your friend, but his product might be
terrific and something that you need. More important, you might see that he's acting out of his own
style needs, just as you do. And maybe he isn't such a
bad guy at all once you get past the superficial differences.

3. *Allow a little ambiguity.* When you find yourself in
a situation with several possible outcomes or approaches, don't avoid it—embrace it! Try living with
the ambivalence and see what happens.

Keep in mind that there's more than one way to
accomplish a task. Did you ever hear the story about
the farmer facing the rising floodwaters? The sheriff's
van came by and offered to rescue the farmer from
his porch, but he said, "No, I'm putting my faith in
the Lord. He'll save me." The sheriff left, and the
flood forced the farmer up onto his roof.

A man with a boat came by, but the farmer said,
"I'll be fine. The Lord will take care of me." After the
rising water forced the farmer atop the chimney, a

helicopter flew over, but the farmer waved it off, citing the same reason.

He drowned and went to heaven where, angrily, he confronted Saint Peter. "What happened?" the farmer asked. "I put my trust in the Lord to save me, and I drowned." Saint Peter replied, "What do you expect? We sent you a sheriff, a boat, and a helicopter. How come you refused all this help God sent you?"

The farmer would have fared better had he not been thinking in such absolute terms. He failed to connect the efforts of his rescuers with his trust in the Lord, to see that the two were not mutually exclusive.

Reconciling two seemingly opposite ideas is not the stretch it sounds like. In fact, it can be the fuel for a lot of creativity. Maybe someone once said, "I want a dessert that's both hot and cold"—and the hot fudge sundae was born! And, then again, perhaps it was baked Alaska. It doesn't matter. The point is: Ambiguity and conflict, if approached with adaptability, can be liberating.

4. *Learn to genuinely listen.* Listening is one of the most important communication skills—and the least taught. Many people assume they are good at it, but few are. Studies show that about three-fourths of what we hear is distorted or quickly forgotten.

In fact, failure to listen well is one of the most frequent causes of misunderstandings, mistakes, and missed opportunities. Poor listening creates tension and distrust, and a cycle is created: If you don't listen, the other person usually stops truly listening, too.

Good listening, on the other hand, can enrich relationships. That's because when you listen to somebody, it makes them feel good about you and themselves. To become a better listener, first focus your attention on the speaker and only on the speaker. Then acknowledge the speaker by nodding, asking questions, or occasionally summarizing his or her statements to show your interest and attention.

Other good-listening tips are to know as much as possible about the speaker's interests and objectives. That will help you ask better questions and communicate on a deeper level. It's also important to exercise emotional control. Regardless of how provocative the message might be, wait until it's received—and understood—before reacting.

Finally, pay attention to the nonverbal language, what's being said with body language, vocal inflection, and gestures. And structure, or organize, the material in your head as you receive it. That will help you retain and understand it better.

5. *Focus first on the positive.* Develop the habit of focusing on the positive dimensions of others (and yourself). Then say something positive before you say something negative.

We could all benefit from viewing people in a more balanced way. If your tendency is to be a fault-finder, tell yourself to "say something positive" before you speak out, and eventually it will become a new habit.

SOME LAST WORDS OF ADVICE

Knowledge, it's said, can be power. Use wisely your new knowledge of the personal styles. Employ the powerful principles of **The Platinum Rule** to understand yourself and others, to improve yourself, and to seek to build rapport with whomever you're with. Distilled to its essence, **The Platinum Rule** equates with "respect for others." It's an attempt to break down the "them versus us" mentality and concentrate on the "us." It's a potent tool for helping you meet the other person's needs *and* your own.

But remember that not everyone knows about the behavioral styles, or even wants to know. And they probably don't want to think they're being categorized by you, either.

So we suggest:

- ✓ Don't show off. Don't try, for instance, to be the hit of the office party by doing a quick, on-the-spot analysis of the personal styles of your boss or co-workers. Be cool, discreet.
- ✓ Be careful about judging someone's style too quickly and making irrevocable decisions based on your perceived compatibility. As we mentioned in the previous chapter, being able to recognize the styles is important, but adapting to them is even more vital. Don't use **The Platinum Rule** to stereotype or limit others.
- ✓ Don't use the concept of the personal styles to excuse your own behavior. (For example, "I'm a Director, so I'm naturally impatient and domineering" or "I can always be forgiven for not following up because I'm a Socializer.") Use **The Platinum Rule** as an insight, not as a crutch.

What **The Platinum Rule** is really about is sensitivity. So, please, use it that way. A person who truly practices the principles of **The Platinum Rule** is more tactful, reasonable, understanding, and non-judgmental.

As long as we live, we'll be dealing with others. **The Platinum Rule** can be used to help us understand and accept ourselves and others. And without such understanding, there can be no appreciation, no love.

That kind of sensitivity, more than ever, is crucial. Collaboration and cooperation loom large as it becomes ever more clear that we are one people living on one planet. Understanding and appreciating differences, therefore, is not merely a technique for better day-to-day living. It's also a vital imperative, and increasingly, a necessity for survival as well, a strength that we must cultivate globally for a more effective lifestyle in the next century.

If you'd like more information about other products and services offered by Alessandra & Associates, contact:

Alessandra & Associates
PO Box 2767
La Jolla, CA 92038-2767
Phone: 619-459-4515
Fax: 619-459-0435
E-Mail: Keyspkr@aol.com
Internet: http://www.alessandra.com